Soldering Demystified

Soldering Demystified

BY JEANETTE K CAINES

Soldering Demystified

Editing by Valerie Blum

Creative Direction and Design by Alexis Idone

Illustrations by Michael Ellis

All Photography by Jeanette K Caines

All Jewelry by Jeanette K Caines except where noted

The Jewelry Arts Institute Way
www.solderingdemystified.com

ISBN-13 978-0615888422

Contents

INTRODUCTION 9

CHAPTER 1 **WHAT IS SOLDERING?** 10

CHAPTER 2 **SOLDERING MATERIALS**

SOLDER 14
SILVER SOLDER 14
GOLD SOLDER 15
FLUX 18
PICKLE 19

CHAPTER 3 **THE RIGHT TOOLS FOR THE JOB**

THE TORCH 22
BOARDS AND BLOCKS 28
TWEEZERS 31
TRIPODS AND SCREENS 31
THE THIRD ARM 32
SHARPIE® PERMANENT MARKER 32

CHAPTER 4 **SET IT UP RIGHT**

CLEAN-UP BEFORE SOLDERING 36
KEEP SOLDERING FLAT AND SUPPORTED 37
GET IN LINE! - THE BEST SOLDERING TIP EVER 38
USING/NOT USING THE THIRD ARM 40

CHAPTER 5 **HEAT IT UP RIGHT : TORCH MYTHS AND REALITIES**

TORCH MYTH #1 : THE HOTTEST PART OF THE FLAME IS THE CONE 46
TORCH MYTH #2 : YOU MUST KEEP THE FLAME MOVING WHILE SOLDERING 46
TORCH MYTH #3 : YOU MUST HEAT THE ENTIRE PIECE WHILE SOLDERING 46
REALITY CHECK : HOW TO HEAT YOUR PIECE CORRECTLY 46

CHAPTER 6 **USE YOUR SOLDER RIGHT : MORE MYTHS AND REALITIES**

SOLDER MYTH #1 : SOLDER WILL NOT FILL GAPS 60
REALITY CHECK : MAKING CAPILLARY ACTION WORK FOR YOU 60
WHERE TO PUT YOUR SOLDER 64
HOW MUCH SOLDER TO USE 64
SOLDER MYTH #2 : USE A SOLDER PICK DURING SOLDERING 69
CLEAN IT UP RIGHT 72

TUTORIAL 1	SOLDERING A VERTICAL SEAM	76
TUTORIAL 2	SOLDERING A BEZEL TO A BACK SHEET	82
TUTORIAL 3	SOLDERING A WIDE SHANK TO A BEZEL	86
TUTORIAL 4	SOLDERING A NARROW SHANK TO A BEZEL	90
TUTORIAL 5	SOLDERING LINKS IN A CHAIN	94
TUTORIAL 6	SOLDERING ON AN EAR WIRE	100
TUTORIAL 7	SOLDERING A POST TO A BEZEL	104
TUTORIAL 8	SOLDERING A JUMP RING TO A BEZEL	108
CONCLUSION		114
GLOSSARY		116
ABOUT THE AUTHOR		119

Introduction

Several years ago, I started offering a soldering workshop to my students. It was called *Soldering: What Are You Doing Wrong?* I gave it that somewhat cheeky title because, in over twenty years of teaching at one of the most prestigious jewelry schools in the country, I realized students had internalized many myths about soldering. As a result, they were making one of a jeweler's most essential skills much harder for themselves. Within each myth is a kernel of truth, misunderstood or misapplied. In the workshop I used my own experience to help students separate myth from reality to make soldering, if not foolproof, at least much easier and more enjoyable.

This book, *Soldering Demystified*, is a compendium of tips and techniques that grew out of that workshop. It is intended for both students and practitioners at every level who wish to improve their soldering skills. I use all of the methods in this book in my own work, and, over the years, have taught them to thousands of students who tell me they continue to use them to this day. I hope they make soldering more simple, successful and fun for you as well.

CHAPTER 1

What Is Soldering?

Soldering is the most all-purpose way to join metal in jewelry and is an ancient and essential skill. Soldered pieces have been found as far back as 5000 BC. In jewelry, the most basic definition of soldering is using a metal (solder) with a lower melting point to join metals with a higher melting point. In other disciplines, this process is called brazing.

Though the concept behind soldering is simple, it also seems to be the most intimidating skill for students. This is understandable, as it involves high heat and manipulation of small components. However, there are some very predictable rules and techniques that can demystify much of soldering. Understanding these, and then practicing - especially the basic soldering operations you will perform repeatedly, such as attaching posts and closing ring shanks, jump rings, bangles, etc. - are the real secrets to successful soldering.

In this book, you will find many practice exercises, along with suggestions for tools, supplies and setups. In addition to providing examples of the best ways to solder, though, I have also endeavored to explain WHY I believe these to be the most effective methods. Understanding the "whys" of soldering will help you build a foundation of knowledge so you can evaluate new soldering scenarios for yourself, and choose the best methods for your work.

Of course, there are many different ways to do things and every studio and instructor will have favorite

CRITERIA FOR THE BEST WAY TO SOLDER

1. Does the technique get the solder to flow every time, quickly?

2. Is the clean-up as minimal as possible?

3. Is there a faster or easier way to set it up?

These questions continue to help me determine the best ways to solder, and can guide you in comparing and developing techniques as well.

methods. Other methods are not "wrong" - but over years of experience, there are many methods I have considered and rejected in favor of techniques I find easier, faster and more effective.

I assume that most readers who pick up this book will have some acquaintance with soldering, but even if you have never soldered before, you can still use it. If you start simple and practice the basic techniques on these pages, you can avoid developing ineffective work habits from the very beginning.

Readers should note that many of my examples show the use of 22k gold and fine (pure) or sterling silver. This is because those are the metals readily on hand in my studio. However, many students make jewelry with brass, copper, sterling silver or 14k or 18k gold. The techniques I discuss will work just as well on these metals. The only modification I suggest for users of these metals, which have a higher copper content and oxidize more than the metals I use, is to apply extra paste flux when soldering.

CHAPTER 2

Soldering Materials

SOLDER

Solder is any metal that melts and flows at a lower temperature than the metals you are joining together. Manufacturers make different solders for silver, gold and other metals so that soldered joints match the color of the metal. In addition, there is usually a variety of different solders within each type of metal. For example, silver solders come in extra hard (IT), hard, medium, easy and extra easy. Extra easy solder has the lowest melting point, and IT (which stands for Intense Temperature) the highest. The range of melting points gives you more control when soldering.

Different companies have slightly different recipes and melting temperatures for each of their solders. Companies will also often provide a temperature range for each solder. The lower number of the range tells you the temperature at which the solder becomes slushy; the higher tells you the temperature at which the solder is completely liquid. It is usually not necessary to know the exact melting points of solder, but it can become important when you are combining different metals with different melting points and want to know what solders can be used safely.

Solder comes in sheet, paste, wire and pre-cut pieces. We use sheet solder exclusively at our studio because it enables us to cut precisely the amount of solder we need.

SILVER SOLDER

Silver solder is by far the most common solder, used on silver, brass and copper, and when combining silver and gold. There are important things to know about each type of silver solder.

EXTRA HARD OR IT (Intense Temperature)

The melting points of IT solder and sterling silver are too close for safe use. IT is used on fine (pure) silver only. Enamelists who work in fine silver favor IT solder because its melting point is higher than that of most enamels and it is less likely to remelt during firing.

HARD

When you are working in sterling silver, hard solder is the one you start with.

MEDIUM

Medium is the most cooperative of the silver solders. Its melting temperature is safely far away from fine

THE GOLDEN (and SILVER) RULE OF SOLDERING

Start with the highest temperature solder your piece can tolerate and work your way down in subsequent soldering operations so your previously soldered joints don't reflow and come apart.

AVERAGE SILVER SOLDER MELTING POINTS

Extra Hard (IT)	1,540°F
Hard	1,475°F
Medium	1,390°F
Easy	1,325°F
Extra Easy	1,300°F

and sterling silver. Because medium solder works so well, I will often use it repeatedly on the same piece. I can get away with that because all previously flowed solders have about a 50°F higher melting point than the unflowed solder of the same type. As a result, as long as a previously soldered seam isn't under any stress from gravity (e.g., suspended up in the air) I can use the same type of solder again and again safely on the same piece. If I'm concerned about remelting a seam (vertical seams are particularly vulnerable), I use ochre (a clay-based soil) or heat sinks to insulate it.

EASY (Soft)

Easy solder is completely misnamed - there is nothing easy about it. It may melt at a low temperature but it is otherwise uncooperative. Rather than flowing toward your heat source, which logic says it should, easy solder will often just puddle up suddenly and make a mess all over your piece. Zinc, which is added in larger and larger quantities to lower the melting point of solder, is the culprit here. It is present in such a large quantity in easy solder that it starts to affect not just melting temperature, but melting behavior. In addition, when overheated, zinc can eat pits into your silver, and the risk of encountering this problem is greatest with easy solder. If you must use it, be particularly prepared to pull the flame away immediately once your solder flows (though that is good advice for all soldering).

EXTRA EASY

Easy solder is so uncooperative we never use extra easy in our studio.

GOLD SOLDER

Gold solders are sold by their karat fineness and in choices of hard, medium, and soft for each karat. There is a small temperature difference among the three choices at each karat. So, in theory, you could step down from 20K hard to 20K medium to 20K soft, getting a progressively lower melting point each time you solder while staying in the 20K category.

Whenever you are using gold solder, remember that you must use an equal or lower karat solder than the karat of the gold in your piece. In other words, if you are soldering together two pieces that are 20K gold, you may start with any 20K solder. You may also use

HELPFUL HINT

Once you have made your informed decision on which silver solder to use, there is nothing worse than accidentally using the wrong solder. At our studio we have a simple system to avoid this: color coding. After we buy and mill our sheets of solder, we take a permanent marker and color in one side of each sheet completely according to the following code:

Black for Extra Hard or IT

Red for Hard

Blue for Medium

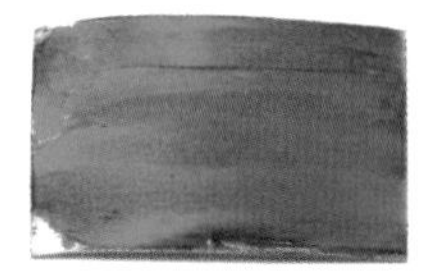

Green for Easy

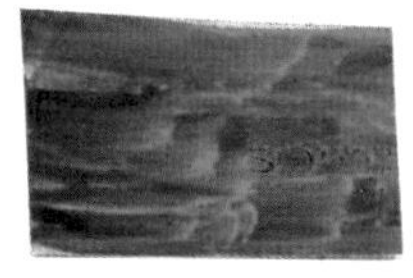

With this method, even if your solder gets mixed up in your tool box, there is no doubt as to what it is.

18K solders, or 14K solders, or any other lower karat solders - though eventually there will be a noticeable color difference between your piece and your solder. What you can NOT do (for example), is use 18K solder on a 14K piece. If you use higher karat solder on a lower karat piece, you will melt your piece before the solder flows.

COMMONLY USED GOLD SOLDERS

22k Hard, Medium, or Soft

20k Hard, Medium, or Soft

18k Hard, Medium, or Soft

14k Hard, Medium, or Soft

12k Hard, Medium, or Soft

10k Hard, Medium, or Soft

8k Hard, Medium, or Soft

Also keep the rule above in mind when you are soldering on findings of a lower karat than your piece. For example, if you are soldering a 14K post to an 18K earring, you must use 14K solder or lower. Bear in mind that lower karat solders get more and more pale and may become very visible on a high-karat piece. Once gold solder gets below the 8K range, the color becomes so washed out it is usually more economical to use silver solder, which has almost the same effect.

In a reversal from the silver solders, the gold easy (i.e., soft) solders are the most cooperative and I tend to use them repeatedly throughout a piece, dispensing entirely with the "medium" and "hard" varieties. For example, in the picture above is a pair of ruby earrings I made with 22k bezels and 20k wire. I used 20k soft again and again to attach all of the decorative wires to the fused bezels. I switched to 18k soft to close all the jump rings between each of the units. Finally, I used 14k soft to attach my 14k posts.

FLUX

Solder only flows successfully when it and the area to be soldered are coated with flux. The word flux comes from the Latin word fluxus, meaning "to flow". That should be a good reminder of how important flux is to keep your solder flowing. Flux is mainly needed because most metals and solders, including sterling silver, brass and gold alloys, are mixed with copper to harden them. In the presence of heat, the copper combines with oxygen to form oxidation. Firescale can also form under the surface of the metal. Flux helps prevent the formation of oxidation and firescale and cleans your metal as you solder.

If you don't use flux, your solder will remain grainy, flow improperly, and possibly overheat and cause pits in your metal. The more copper in the metal you are working with, the more oxidation - so use more flux on metals with a high copper content, such as sterling silver, 14k gold, brass or copper itself.

PASTE FLUX TIP

Using paste flux that is too dry can make it surprisingly difficult to get the solder to let go of the tweezers, so don't neglect to add some water in your paste flux and stir it around at the beginning of every bench session.

RIGHT
Flux is watery and will "let go" of my tweezers when I decide it should.

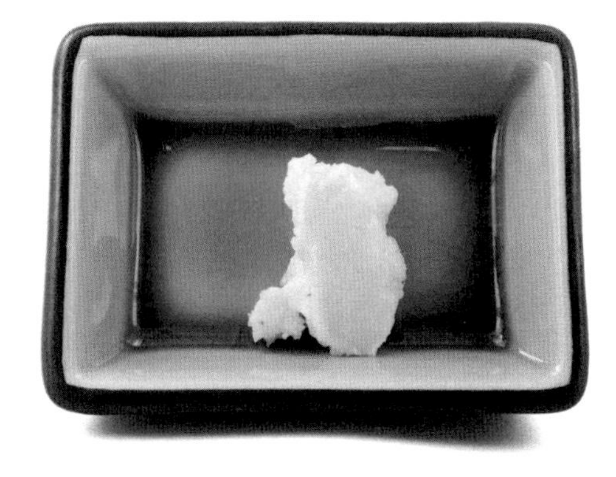

WRONG
Flux is dry and hard to work with. Add warm water and stir to make it more manageable.

The flux I most commonly use is paste flux. Paste flux is more concentrated than liquid flux and more precise to apply than spray, and I find it to be extremely effective.

My preferred method for applying paste flux is to mix it with water to a watery consistency, dip my solder ball into it and then put it where I want it. This is often enough to keep the solder in place, and much faster than the textbook technique of fluxing and drying the whole piece first and then placing the solder afterward. If I need my piece of solder to stay exactly where I put it (as when I am soldering the connection between a bezel and a jump ring), I heat the piece a bit and then dip and place my solder ball with my stone tweezers. When the piece is a little warm, the flux dries instantly and "glues" the solder to the spot. Because I sometimes warm the piece before applying flux, I don't use flux brushes - unlike stainless steel tweezers, the bristles of the brush will burn if they come in contact with hot metal.

Fluxes other than paste flux can also be useful. Firescoff®, a spray-on ceramic coating that prevents oxidation and also contains flux, is helpful for uses like repeated soldering on a large object prone to oxidation and fire scale. (e.g., a sterling silver cuff) because it coats the entire piece and eliminates the need to pickle between operations. Firescoff® is the first innovation in flux in 3500 years and it's use in a variety of jewelry applications continues to expand and is still being explored. Liquid flux performs the same basic functions as paste flux but is less concentrated and less effective in extended heating situations.

PICKLE

Pickle is a dilute acid solution used to clean off oxidation and spent flux after soldering. At our school, we use a solution of a common swimming pool additive (Ph minus) as our pickle. The chemical name of the pickle we use is sodium bisulfate. The ratio of dry sodium bisulfate to water in the solution we use is about 1:8. Just in case you mix your own pickle and do not remember your chemistry classes, be sure to add the dry acid granules to your container of water, rather than vice versa! If you do it the other way around and add water to the acid granules, you can create a violent and dangerous reaction that can spray you with concentrated acid solution.

We use our pickle warm (not boiling!) and keep it in covered ceramic (not metal!) commercial slow cookers that sit under a hooded vent to keep irritating pickle vapor out of the air. Warm pickle works faster than cold pickle; hot pickle just steams into the air and degrades air quality without substantially speeding up the pickling process. In the warm solution, it usually takes about three to five minutes for an object to get fully cleaned, though times may vary depending on the temperature and strength of the pickle, and the amount of flux and oxidation on the piece.

How long your pickle solution will last depends on how many people are using it. My pickle in my home studio with only one user will often last for many months, but the pickle in a busy studio with many jewelers will get used up faster. It's pretty obvious when you need to change the pickle, as it will start to take longer and longer to clean objects, even when the pickle is warm. When this happens, take it to a sink or toilet and add a few teaspoons of baking soda to neutralize it (it will foam up and may overflow your container, so be careful). Once the solution stops foaming, flush it down the toilet.

Only copper tweezers should be used to take objects in and out of the pickle. Steel tweezers (or binding wire or any other ferrous metal) will react with the pickle on contact, causing the copper dissolved in the solution to

HELPFUL HINT

A common myth is that once copper plating has happened in the pickle, the pickle is "contaminated" and needs to be discarded. This is untrue. The copper plating ceases to occur once the steel has been removed from the solution, and can be removed from your piece by applying paste flux, heating and pickling again.

plate your piece and everything else in the pickle pot.

The main reason to pickle after a soldering operation is to clear away flux and oxidation so that you can see whether your solder seam has filled completely. That

Do not quench hot jewelry in the pickle.

This sprays hot pickle everywhere, which will make holes in your clothes. In addition, the spray from this bad habit can eventually eat through your slow cooker's power cord, causing an electrical fire hazard.

said, when it is obvious that you need to add another ball of solder to a well-fluxed joint, or are soldering a second time in an area that is far from your first soldering operation, you don't need to pickle in between. Using paste flux usually enables you to add more solder with fresh paste flux without pickling. Eventually, experience will tell you when it is OK to skip a trip to the pickle. When in doubt, err on the safe side and just do it.

Once an object is fully pickled, it should be rinsed with water. If there are any hollow areas in the piece that could trap the liquid pickle, you should take the extra step of submerging the object in a heated solution of water and baking soda to neutralize any pickle inside the hollow spaces.

CHAPTER 3

The Right Tools for the Job

There are many different tools to choose from when soldering jewelry. Over the years, I have found some that I think make the process much easier. This chapter gives an overview of some of the basic tools and equipment I recommend – with a few do's and don'ts along the way.

THE TORCH

All torches burn some kind of fuel. Some studios use propane, some use natural gas and some use acetylene. Jewelers doing repairs, working in platinum, or performing other work that requires a very small but very hot flame may use a system with separate oxygen and gas tanks, providing a flame that can burn at temperatures up to 6,000 degrees Fahrenheit. At the other end of the spectrum are home jewelers who use hand-held butane torches. These burn at about 2,000 degrees Fahrenheit and are suitable for making small pieces of jewelry, but not for fabricating large pieces or for alloying metals.

My personal favorite torch, which we use at the Jewelry Arts Institute, is an acetylene and atmospheric oxygen torch. This is a straight acetylene tank with no additional oxygen tank. Because there is only one tank and only one gas control valve, this is a very simple and safe system to use. The flame burns at a maximum of about 3,000 degrees Fahrenheit - ample heat for the soldering and alloying we do.

Acetylene has acquired a bad (and, in my opinion, somewhat undeserved) reputation in certain sources. Occasionally, I come across a book that claims acetylene is a "dirty" gas and produces soot. While this is technically true and an acetylene flame is not appropriate for working in platinum, I have never had any trouble working with it on gold, silver, brass or copper, or seen it produce any soot on these metals, and my students and I use it without difficulty. Whatever gas you use, though, the most important thing is that you understand how it works and what safety precautions to take.

TORCH SAFETY

Jewelry torches are very safe if used properly but should always be treated with respect. If you have ANY doubt about how to use your torch or what kind of setup you are using, ask your instructor or studio monitor for help. Only when you are completely versed in torch safety and maintenance AND know what to do in case of ANY emergency should you consider having a torch in your own studio.

MELTING POINTS OF IMPORTANT METALS

Metal	Melting point
Copper	1984° F
22k Yellow Gold	1930° F
18k Yellow Gold	1700° F
14k Yellow Gold	1615° F
Fine (Pure) Silver	1761° F
Sterling Silver	1640° F
Brass	1650-1724° F

Remember, when you are soldering you will not be getting any of these metals to their melting point (you hope!). The melting temperature of solder for any particular metal is usually at least a couple of hundred degrees less than of the metal itself.

IMPORTANT!

Here are a few critical safety rules you should always remember. These tips may sound obvious, however, every torch problem I have ever seen has resulted from a failure to follow one of these rules.

1. If your eyes are not on the flame, turn it off.

2. Every time you pick up the torch to use it, check that the tip is tightly attached. Torch tips can loosen and eventually fall off, creating a major fire hazard.

3. Make sure the flame is completely out before you set your torch down.

TORCH BASICS

At our studio, we use a Smith torch handle kit. To light our torch, we simply turn on the gas and ignite it with a striker. To vary the size of the flame, we change the tip to a larger or smaller size. Different torch handle manufacturers have their own numbering system for torch tips, and the numbering system may also vary depending on the kind of gas used. To avoid confusion, I have photographed the tips I use most often with their flame measured against a ruler. If you use a different system, the guide on the facing page can help you determine which of your tips provides a comparable flame.

Pictured from left to right are the Smith tips 2, 1, 0, and 00.

TORCH SIZE GUIDE

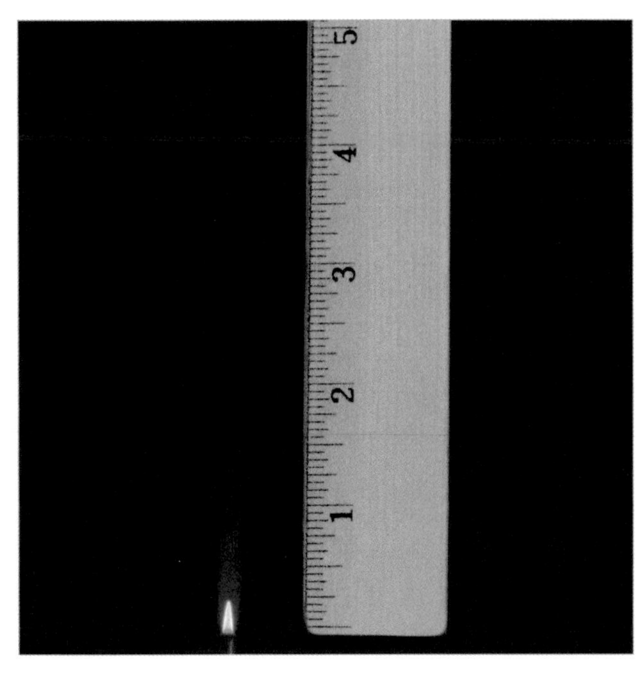

00 tip. Flame is 1 to 1 1/2 inches (about 25-40 mm) long. Use for small soldering jobs such as attaching posts or ear wires or soldering jump rings.

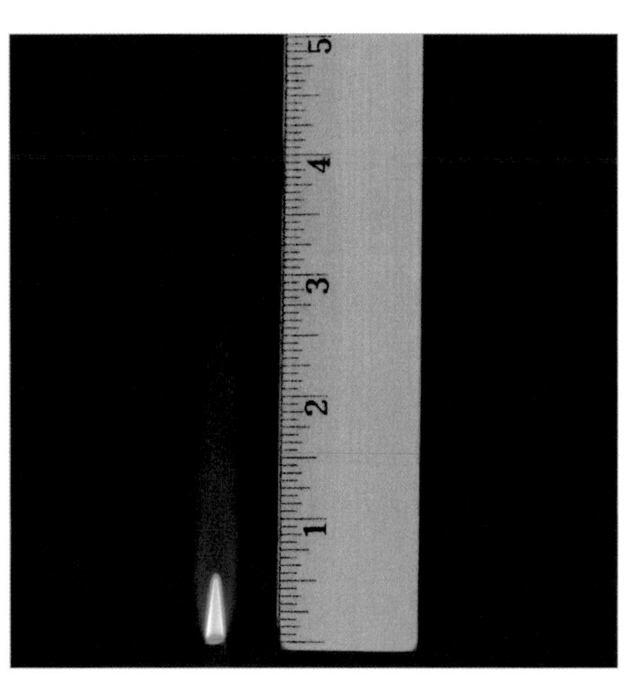

0 tip. Flame is 3-4 inches (about 75-100mm) long. This is the tip I use most often for closing ring shanks and soldering bezels to back sheets, shanks to settings, etc.

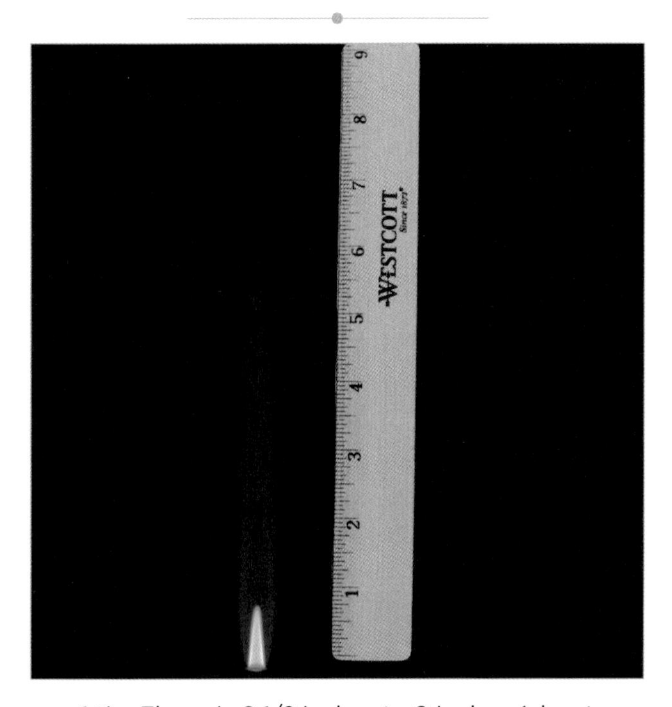

1 tip. Flame is 6 1/2 inches to 9 inches (about 16 cm-23 cm) long. Use for larger soldering jobs, such as bracelets and cuffs, etc.

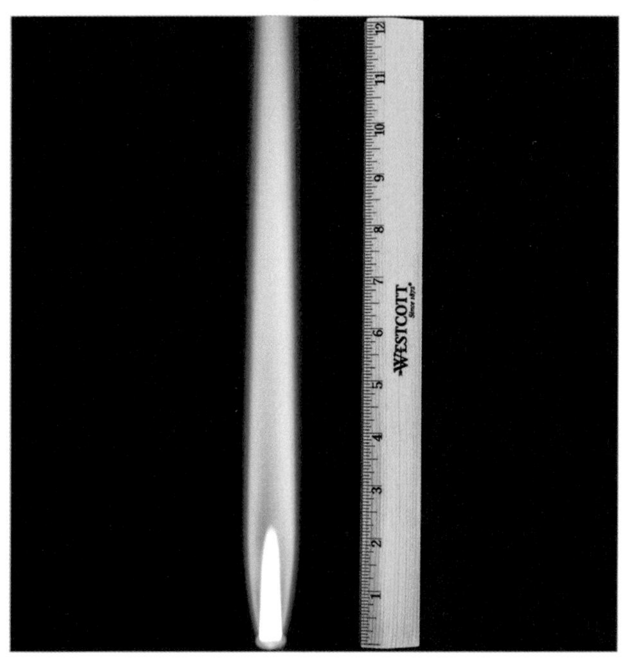

2 tip. Flame is 14 inches to 16 inches (about 36 cm-41 cm) long. Use for alloying gold, and soldering very large pieces.

BOARDS AND BLOCKS

There are numerous boards and blocks available for soldering. Fortunately, these (and many other soldering tools) are relatively inexpensive. A corollary of this, though, is that they can and should be replaced fairly often. Below is a brief discussion of the boards and blocks I use most often and what yours should - and should not - look like.

CHARCOAL BLOCKS

I use charcoal blocks for techniques that involve fully melting the metal, such as alloying and making granules. In these cases, a Solderite block is less than ideal because the white surface sticks to the metal when it melts, creating white, crunchy deposits. In addition, it is much easier to dig into a charcoal block to create depressions for alloying, and for catching granules before they roll off the block and into your lap.

A charcoal block can also be used for soldering and fusing, but I prefer the Solderite board because it maintains a flat surface significantly longer than the charcoal block. Charcoal also leaves black dust everywhere.

The picture on the top right is a block well past its prime. Charcoal blocks end up looking like this because they get coated with flux, and because they are combustible and burn and smolder, just like charcoal on a barbecue. You can prolong the life of a charcoal block by wetting it down with clean water once you are finished using it, but at some point, you need to know when to let go. An easy soldering job can become almost impossible when you are working on a dirty, uneven surface such as this. See facing page, top right ›.

SOLDERITE BOARDS

One of my favorite soldering surfaces is a new, clean Solderite board. The surface is flat and clean to work on, and the pieces to be soldered are highly visible against the white background. Solderite boards also reflect more heat than any other block I have used and I believe I have tried them all. The greatest benefit of using a Solderite board is the clean, flat surface it provides. So... if your Solderite board looks like the picture on the right, don't use it for soldering! It can still be used for annealing and propping things up, but it should be retired from active soldering duty. See facing page, bottom right ›.

CHARCOAL BLOCKS

Good

Time to retire

SOLDERITE BOARDS

Good

Time to retire

Good

Time to retire

MAGNESIA BLOCKS

The main advantage of a Magnesia block is that it is soft, allowing you to press work down into it while soldering, see image, bottom right. The block will hold some or all of the parts you are soldering in place, making setup much easier. You can also insert soldering aids, such as binding wire or straight pins, into a Magnesia block. In theory you can also do this with charcoal, but in practice I find it messy, creating lots of dirty bits of charcoal block in your soldering area.

Another advantage to a Magnesia block is that you can press a partially finished piece, such as an earring, into it to protect the previously soldered seam. Alternatively, ochre can be painted on the seam, but this alone is not enough to protect that seam if it is up in the air, so the magnesia block is a better option. Another solution for protecting the seam would be to use a third arm, which is a pair of freestanding tweezers on a base, but this is annoying and fiddly to do (more on this later). Once you get used to the Magnesia block, you will find numerous applications for it and wonder how you ever lived without it.

Because they are soft, Magnesia blocks are especially vulnerable to crumbling and decomposition. If your Magnesia block looks like the picture above, you can try to restore its flat surfaces by going over it with a coarse file or rasp. This creates a lot of white dust, so I suggest wearing a mask. You will also have a lot of white powder to clean out of your file when you are done – and your block will get smaller each time you level it. You will need to replace these blocks on a fairly regular basis.

Tripod with screen

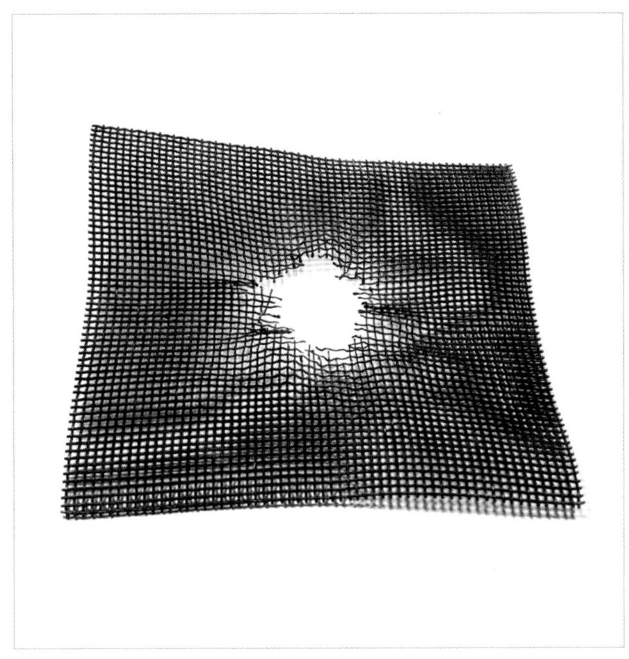

Screen

TWEEZERS

Believe it or not, to place and move small pieces of solder I use tweezers and only tweezers - not a solder pick. I'll explain more about why later, but for now, suffice it to say that I recommend stone or diamond tweezers for soldering. This is because they are pointy enough to pick up small pieces of solder, and their texture, which is meant to grip small stones, also turns out to be perfect for holding tiny solder balls. In addition, they hold up well when subjected to heat.

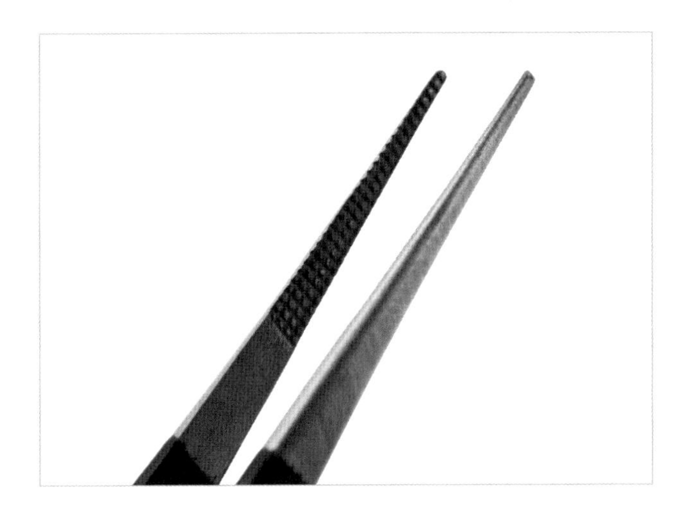

For soldering, I don't buy really expensive tweezers meant for very fine stones - the $10-or-less variety works just fine - and I always keep several on my bench. They grab and hold solder - as well as small jump rings, posts and other components - just as well as more expensive tweezers. I don't worry about "ruining" them while soldering because, as far as I am concerned, soldering is one of the main jobs tweezers should be used for! When they get sticky with flux, I just rinse them off. When they get really grungy, I buy another pair. It's worth it when you think about the time and effort they save.

TRIPODS AND SCREENS

The purpose of a tripod and screen is to enable you to heat from below, rather than above as on a board or block. A key principle of soldering, which will be discussed in detail in future chapters, is that solder flows toward the source of heat. Heating from below is crucial in many soldering operations when you want to pull your solder downward or around rather than up.

Soldering a bezel to a back sheet provides a prime

example of when to use a tripod rather than a block. If you set the back sheet on a block and place the bezel on top, you must by necessity heat the piece from somewhere above it, which can pull the solder up the sides of the bezel. A tripod enables you to position the heat below the back sheet, pulling your solder down and around the seam where it belongs.

You may be surprised when I tell you that if your screen looks like the one on the previous page, you shouldn't throw it out! There is a point of no return for screens, but this isn't it - despite the bumps and the hole in the center. If the bumps interfere with your soldering, you can gently tap them out with a leather mallet. Screens can also act as heat sinks, so make sure you buy a thin one, rather than a thick one, for soldering on your tripod - and don't worry if a hole develops since it will actually allow more heat to get to your piece.

THE THIRD ARM

A third arm is nothing more than a cross-locking tweezer in a stand. Most of the time, we use it to hold one component right up against another when we are soldering them together. For example, we use a third arm to hold a post when we solder it onto an earring, or to hold a narrow shank when we solder it onto a bezel.

Third arms can be difficult to use. You will most certainly find that it takes far longer to set up (i.e., straighten and center) a piece in a third arm than it does to solder it. As a result, the best advice regarding the third arm is to avoid it wherever possible. Anything that can be pressed into a Magnesia block, or laid flat and soldered together on a Solderite board, or placed up on a tripod, should be. Unfortunately, though, there is sometimes no substitute, so you should include a third arm in your repertoire of soldering tools.

SHARPIE® PERMANENT MARKER

Although a Sharpie marker is not technically a jewelry tool I use it quite a bit in my studio. It is perfect for making a mark that will completely disappear during soldering so I use it to mark where I want various components. It works well on all but the most precise mechanisms, where you must use a divider. A Sharpie marker's color disappears at around 1100°F so it is also helpful for annealing. Annealing is the process of heating metal to make it malleable and many students find it difficult to know if they have heated their metal too much or too little. The annealing range of most jewelry metals is between 1150°F and 1250°F so once your Sharpie marker color disappears heat it for another second or so and your metal is perfectly annealed.[1]

BEFORE ANNEALING

Make a mark (or silly drawing) on your metal that needs annealing. Heat with a torch or in the kiln until the color disappears. Your metal is annealed.

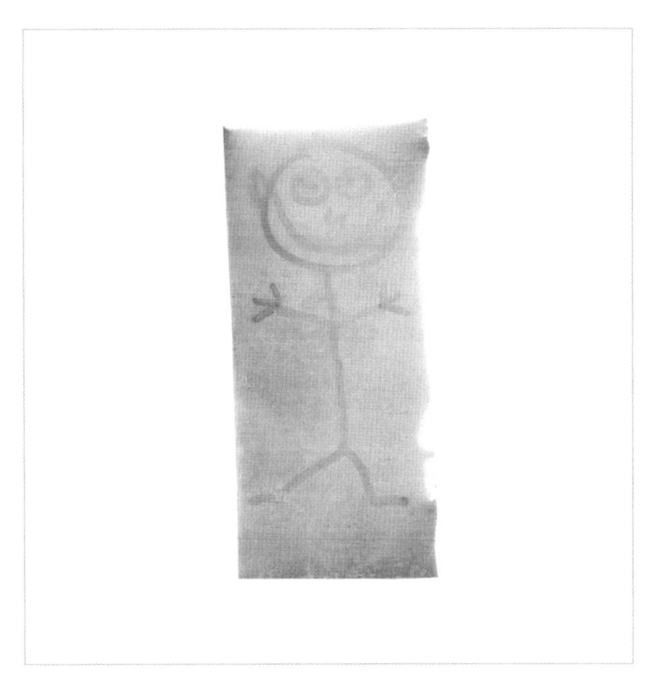

AFTER ANNEALING

Your metal may show a "ghost" of your drawing if viewed from just the right angle. Don't worry, it will disappear as you continue to work with your metal.

CHAPTER 4

Set It Up Right

Why won't my solder flow? Why did my post fall off? How did I melt my piece?

If you think you did everything right, yet continue to encounter frustrating soldering mishaps, read on. This chapter will guide you through key elements of the soldering process, from proper setup to proper heating to proper clean-up, that can eliminate much soldering anxiety and set you on the path to soldering more quickly, efficiently and happily.

CLEAN-UP BEFORE SOLDERING

Except in very rare cases, it is best to clean-up all elements you are attaching before you solder them together. In my experience, the "I'll clean it up at the end!" approach takes twice as long and ends up looking half as good. This applies to sanding and removing scratches before soldering, and to soldering neatly, with the right amount of solder in the right places to avoid messy joints requiring lots of clean-up later (see Use Your Solder Right for more).

Cleaning up your pieces before soldering means they are sanded and filed to fit together well, and then finished to a degree that will allow you to do little more than a final sand-polish job at the end. Often, once two pieces are connected, you will find it is almost impossible to get between them with a file or sandpaper to clean them up. If you see a scratch on a piece before you solder, get rid of it then, rather than after you have attached another piece right next to it and blocked your access.

To clean-up components before soldering, first file if you have any major bumps and scratches. (Be careful when you file – if you dig away only in the area over a scratch, you will carve a deep and visible trench, so file carefully and evenly to blend the filed area with the entire piece.) Then, progress from coarse to finer sandpapers, depending on the finish you want. When I clean-up pieces, I personally don't like to start with a file more coarse than a Swiss cut 2, after which I proceed to 400 sandpaper, and finally to micron graded 400 sandpaper, which gives a more even finish. I then consider my piece ready to solder.

SCRATCHING THE SURFACE: THE TRUTH ABOUT POLISHING

If you haven't thought about it, you might not realize that filing, sanding and polishing are all just progressive steps in the process of removing larger visible scratches, and replacing them with a surface of smaller scratches, all of the same depth. If your scratches are not all the same depth, the deeper scratches become easier and easier to see the more you polish. For this reason, you should never progress to a finer sandpaper before you have taken out all possible scratches with the sandpaper you are using. For example, if you are using 400 sandpaper to take out file marks, don't decide you are done and switch to 600 sandpaper while you can still see those file marks! If you do this, all you will get are a lot of highly polished file marks and you will have to go back and do everything over to remove them.

KEEP SOLDERING FLAT AND SUPPORTED

The easiest set-up for soldering is to have as much support as possible for the pieces you are attaching. Pieces that are suspended up in the air from third arms, or sticking out of (Messy! Scratchy!) grit bowls, are highly vulnerable to melting and reflow of previously soldered seams. Components that are not flat and supported are also much more likely to end up getting soldered on crooked. As you read this chapter, you will notice that every soldering set-up that follows is as flat and supported as possible, utilizing a Solderite board or Magnesia block wherever feasible.

A grit bowl forces pieces to be soldered unsupported above the surface of the grit. Avoid this when possible. It is most useful for soldering or annealing large curved objects that cannot be supported in other ways.

The magnesia block allows you to embed and fully support both your bezel and your jump ring. Always opt to avoid using the messy grit bowl and the fussy third arm.

GET IN LINE! THE BEST SOLDERING TIP EVER

How many times have you soldered on a finding you thought was perfectly lined up with the rest of your piece, only to find it is several degrees off center? (And why does this become so easily visible only after you have soldered it on?) Aligning elements for soldering is one of the biggest obstacles confronted by students and professionals alike, and yet the problem has a really easy solution. In fact, when this idea finally occurred to me about ten years ago, my first thought was, "what took me so long?"! When I made a video about it for the Jewelry Arts Institute's YouTube channel, I called it *The Best Jewelry Soldering Tip Ever*, and I still believe that to be true.

Here it is in three easy steps:

1 Get a new Solderite board and line up the end of a metal ruler with the edge of your board. Draw the line using a ballpoint pen (the X axis).

Note: Ballpoint pens write best on this surface.

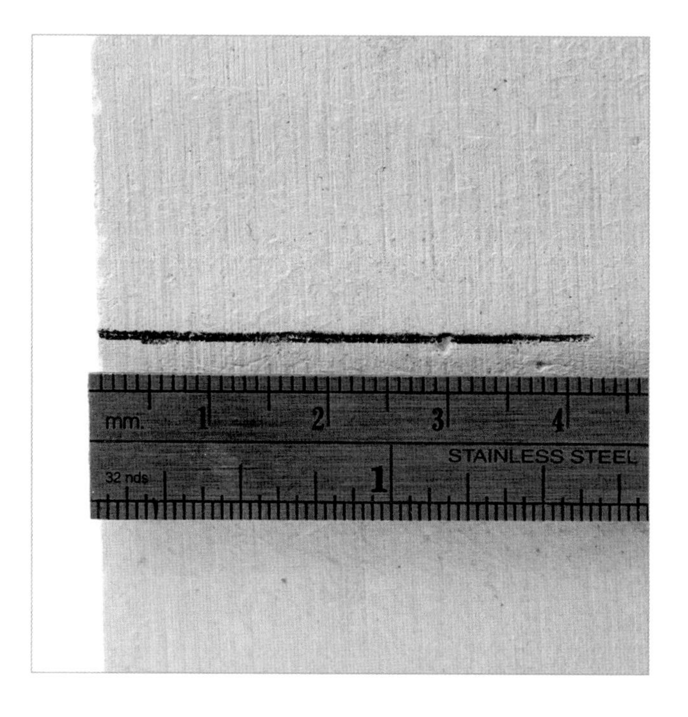

2 Line up the edge of your ruler with the bottom edge of your block, at 90° to the first line, and draw this line with your pen (the Y axis).

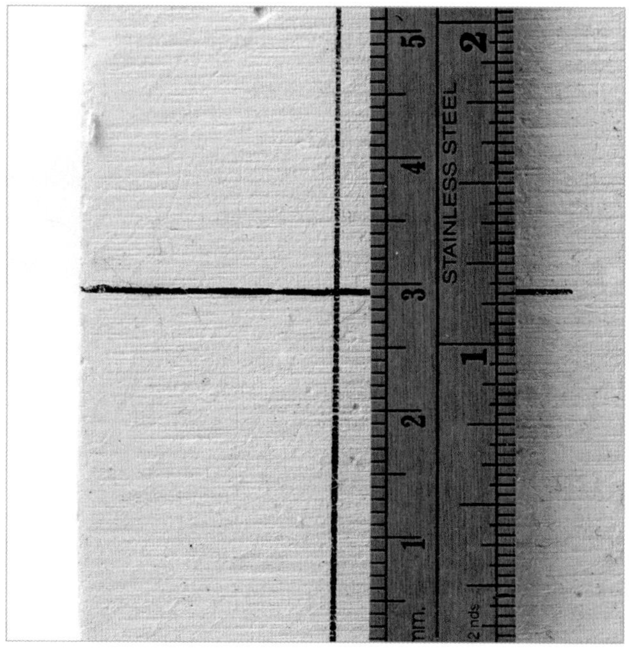

3

For more complicated setups, use an angle ruler to draw in 4 more lines at 45 degree angles to your first lines. (Your lines will fade with use, so freshen them up occasionally.)

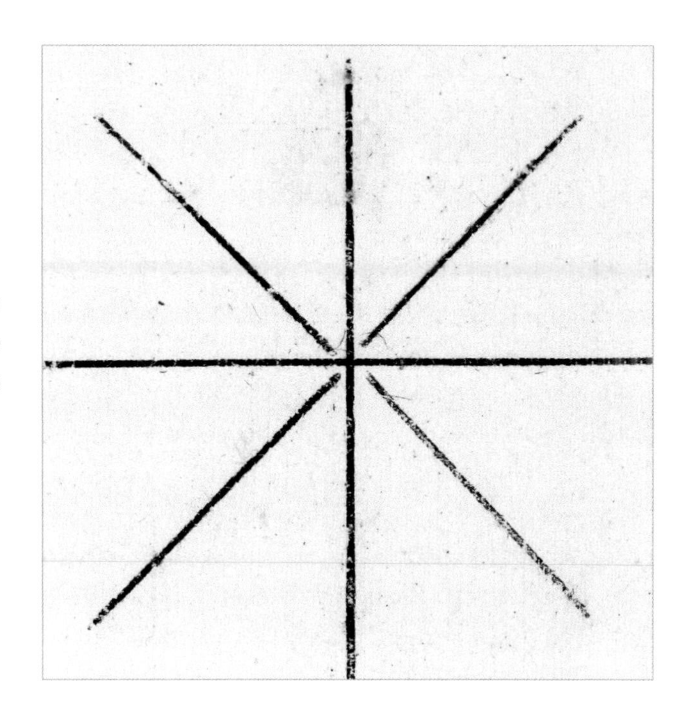

Examples:

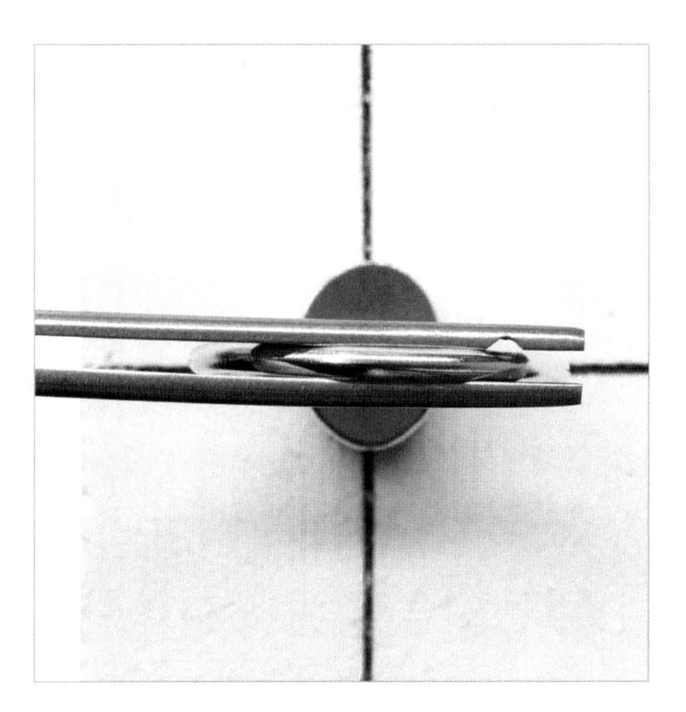

The 90° lines work for straightforward soldering setups.

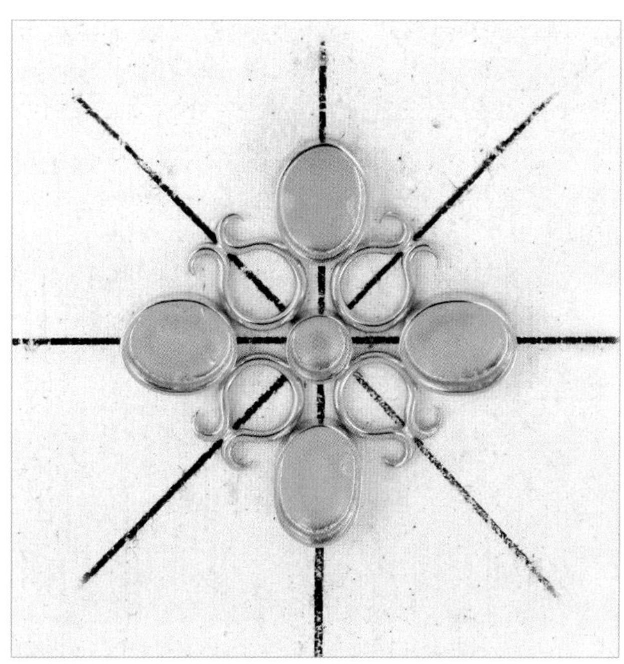

You can use this setup for more complicated soldering arrangements.

USING/NOT USING THE THIRD ARM

If you read the section on tools already, you might remember these words: the best advice regarding the third arm is to avoid it wherever possible. But why? Here are just a few reasons:

Third arms are made to rotate in all directions. So, in addition to making sure things are centered, you also have to check from all angles to see if what you're holding in the third arm (e.g., a jump ring) isn't tilted forward or backward, or twisted a few degrees to one side or the other. And if that's not annoying enough, third arms can be very difficult to manipulate. They are either so stiff they jerk out of position when you try to move them, or so loose that the tweezers end up falling out while you are in the middle of setting up. If you use a flat Solderite board or Magnesia block to line up your pieces when possible, you avoid these problems.

In addition, improper use of the third arm can result in total collapse of a hollow piece. NEVER clamp a third arm around anything hollow or partially hollow, such as a bezel that has been soldered to a back sheet. If it gets hot enough, the force of the cross locking tweezer can crush your object. I've seen it happen and it isn't pretty.

Finally, because they are made of steel, which has a much higher melting point than gold or silver, third arms can act as heat sinks, meaning they can draw a lot of heat away from your piece and into themselves. Often, when solder refuses to flow properly it is because of the third arm. You can use this feature to your advantage - for example, you can protect a previously soldered seam from reflow by clamping the third arm over it - but you need to know how to position the third arm properly when you do need your solder to flow unimpeded.

DANGER!
This piece may well get crushed during soldering.

* * *

IMPORTANT!

Yes, they're annoying, but yes, you have to use them sometimes. Where you have no other choice, remember the following points regarding third arms:

1. Always clamp your object as far away as possible from your solder seam.

2. After setting up your piece in the third arm, get up and check from all angles. Things that look perfectly straight from the front may look very different when viewed from the side.

3. Never clamp anything hollow or partially hollow in the third arm.

RIGHT
This setup will help the soldering go quickly.

WRONG
A third arm positioned this close to the solder joint will absorb heat and can impede solder flow.

HOW TO USE THE THIRD ARM

RIGHT : The third arm is positioned as far away as possible from the solder.

WRONG : The third arm is too close to the soldering joint.

RIGHT : The third arm positioned at the top portion of the jump ring will help the soldering go quickly.

WRONG : If too much of the jump ring is covered the solder won't flow to it.

CHAPTER 5

Heat it Up Right: Torch Myths and Realities

We've now talked about setting up and lining up your components for soldering. But successful soldering also requires knowing how solder behaves once heat is applied. There are many myths about heating pieces during soldering that filter down to students and cause innumerable problems during relatively simple soldering operations. As you read the following sections, remember the three key points about heating during soldering:

IMPORTANT!

1. Hot and fast is the key. Solder will not flow if it does not get hot enough, fast enough.

2. Heat is like a magnet, and solder will flow to the hottest area of your piece first.

3. Clean, well-fitted pieces and adequate flux are essential for good solder flow.

These points will guide us again and again in separating myth from reality, and determining where, how and why to heat a piece.

HELPFUL HINT

I never flux my solder squares before I ball them up. If you heat them quickly and use paste flux while soldering, the unfluxed balls work perfectly. Fluxing them before balling makes your soldering board a crunchy mess.

HOW TO USE A TORCH

The blue cone of the flame may be the hottest part of the flame but it won't help you during soldering.

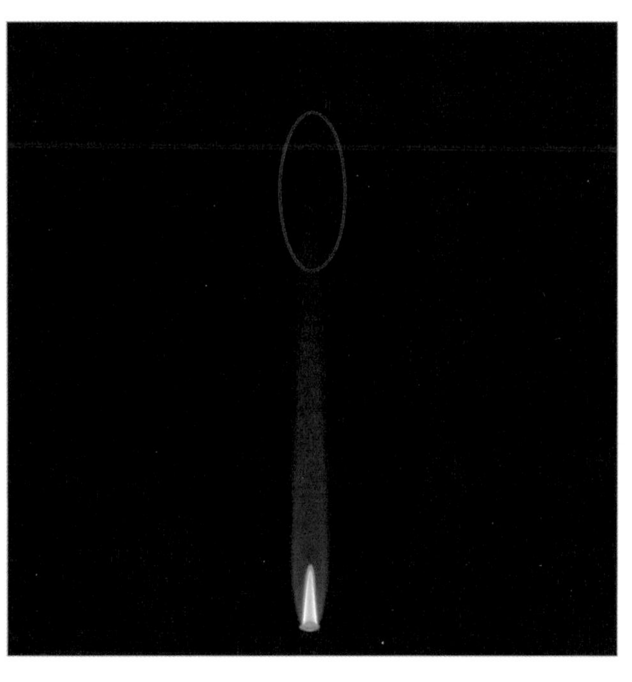

The end of the flame. This is the part of the flame to use while soldering.

RIGHT : Position the end of the flame on your piece.

WRONG : Much of your flame's heat will be released beyond your piece if you use this position.

TORCH MYTH #1 - THE HOTTEST PART OF THE FLAME IS THE CONE

You may have read or heard that the hottest part of the flame is the little bluish cone. Although I am sure that if you checked the separate parts of the flame with a high-heat thermometer this would be correct, it is not helpful for soldering. When you are actually using the torch, all of the heat is heading toward the end or tip of the flame. If you try to position the cone near what you are trying to heat, then most of the flame's heat is actually released beyond your piece and doing you no good at all.

When you solder, position the end of your flame on what you are trying to heat. This will get your piece hotter, faster. Hot and fast are essential to successful soldering. You cannot heat your piece adequately and quickly enough if you attempt to use the cone of the flame for soldering. Using the end of the torch tip also gives you greater control. You can pull your flame away faster when you use the tip rather than the cone of the flame.

TORCH MYTH #2 - YOU MUST KEEP THE FLAME MOVING WHILE SOLDERING

Remember hot and fast? You will achieve neither if you are constantly jiggling or circling your flame while soldering. The longer it takes to get your piece to soldering temperature, the more time there is for the metal to oxidize and your solder to get dirty and refuse to flow.

No teacher wants a student to melt a piece, and I believe that's probably why the conventional wisdom of "keep the flame moving" keeps circulating. Also, this advice probably originated with jewelers using much larger or hotter torch flames than the ones I recommend in this book. When we solder, we want hot and fast, but we also need control. All the heat in the world won't help your soldering unless YOU are in control of it. I have witnessed thousands of soldering operations done by students using an acetylene torch, and can testify that the main problem is that they don't get the piece hot enough, fast enough. When students do melt a piece it is usually because they fail to see that the solder has already flowed and continue to heat the piece. Remember that solder flows at a lower temperature than your metal so, as long as you keep an eye on your solder and pull the heat away as soon as it melts, you shouldn't have a problem.

TORCH MYTH #3 - YOU MUST HEAT THE ENTIRE PIECE WHILE SOLDERING

Another fallacy is that you must heat the entire piece to solder. This is not true, particularly if your piece is large, like a bracelet. What must get hot is the seam you are trying to fill, NOT the entire piece. You can't get your seam hot enough to solder while you are going around and around the whole piece; too much of the heat will dissipate. What you must do instead is keep your torch positioned near the seam you are trying to fill. Once again, hot and fast is the key. You will be amazed how quickly and beautifully your solder flows when you aim the heat near the place you are soldering, rather than circling around it.

Another way to think about this is to recall the second key point about soldering from the start of this section: Heat is like a magnet, and solder will flow to the hottest area of your piece first. Rather than revolving around and around a piece to heat it up, you need to strategically position your heat in the place it will do the most good (i.e., where it will draw the solder into the gap you are trying to fill).

REALITY CHECK: HOW TO HEAT YOUR PIECE CORRECTLY

Those are the myths, but what are the realities of heating your piece? Where do you hold your flame when soldering?

The most simple formulation of the rule of where to heat your piece is something we mentioned earlier in this section: solder always flows toward the hottest part of your piece. As a result, you should position your solder and torch so that you are using the heat to pull the solder through whatever gap you are trying to fill. Often, this means putting solder on one side and heating from the other. Another way to get the solder into the gap you are trying to fill is by "sandwiching" the solder between the two components.

When one part of a soldering setup is significantly smaller than the other, (e.g., a post or jump ring), the small piece can easily become hotter than the larger piece. Once that happens, the solder will "jump" onto the smaller piece and make a mess, rather than filling the gap between the two components. You might even melt the smaller piece before the solder flows. The solution to this is to position your torch on the larger of the two components. Generally speaking, the smaller part gets hot enough just being in the vicinity of the heat.

HOW TO HEAT YOUR PIECE CORRECTLY

RIGHT : Heat the larger of the two components so solder will flow between the two.

WRONG : Heating the jump ring directly will cause the solder to only melt to the jump ring.

RIGHT : Only heating the bezel will make the solder flow successfully.

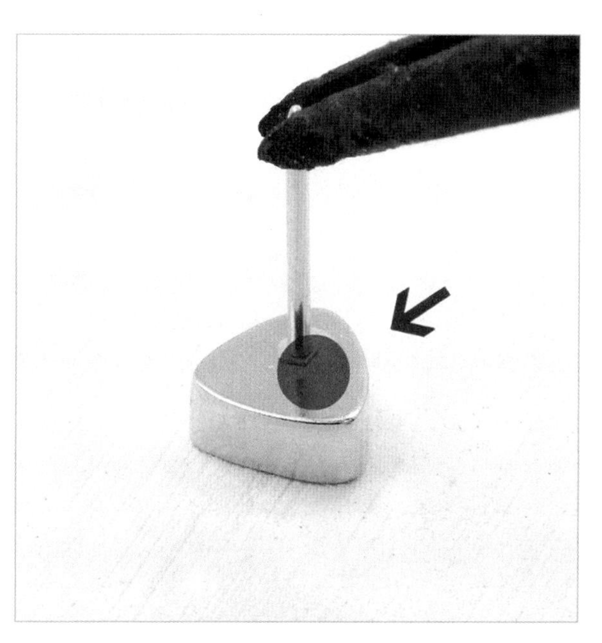

WRONG : Heating the post directly may cause a melted post.

How these techniques come together in these Rubellite earrings:

First I soldered my fused bezels down to their separate back sheets up on a tripod using 20k soft gold solder balls. I shaped my decorative 20k gold wires and soldered them shut flat on my Solderite board, also using 20k soft gold solder balls. After the bezels were completely filed, sanded and cleaned, I aligned them from the center bezel out on my marked Solderite board along with my wires (see pictures of this method to the right). I soldered my bezels to my wires using 18k soft gold solder. I used 18k soft gold solder again to close the jump ring between the two units, pressed them top down into a Magnesia block and switched down to 14k soft gold solder to attach the 14k gold post to the top bezel. Using these soldering methods results in very little clean-up, so I just used a bit of fine sandpaper and then tumbled before setting the stones.

When I am soldering on an ear wire, I position my flame at 90° to the earring to prevent the flame from making contact with (and melting) my ear wire. I am heating the larger piece (the earring) not the smaller piece (the ear wire), which I deliberately aim to miss.

RIGHT : Heating only the earring will make the solder flow beautifully.

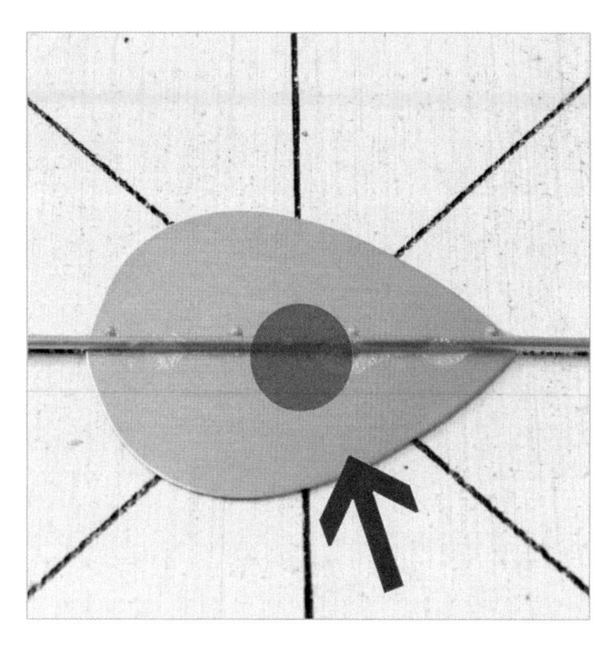

WRONG : Letting the flame touch the ear wire will likely melt the ear wire.

If I am soldering together two elements that are more equal in mass, I position my flame on both parts. If I heat one piece more than the other in such a case, the solder will "jump" to the hotter side, so heat equal-sized pieces equally.

RIGHT : Heat both pieces when elements are more equally sized.

WRONG : This can cause solder to flow on only one of the pieces.

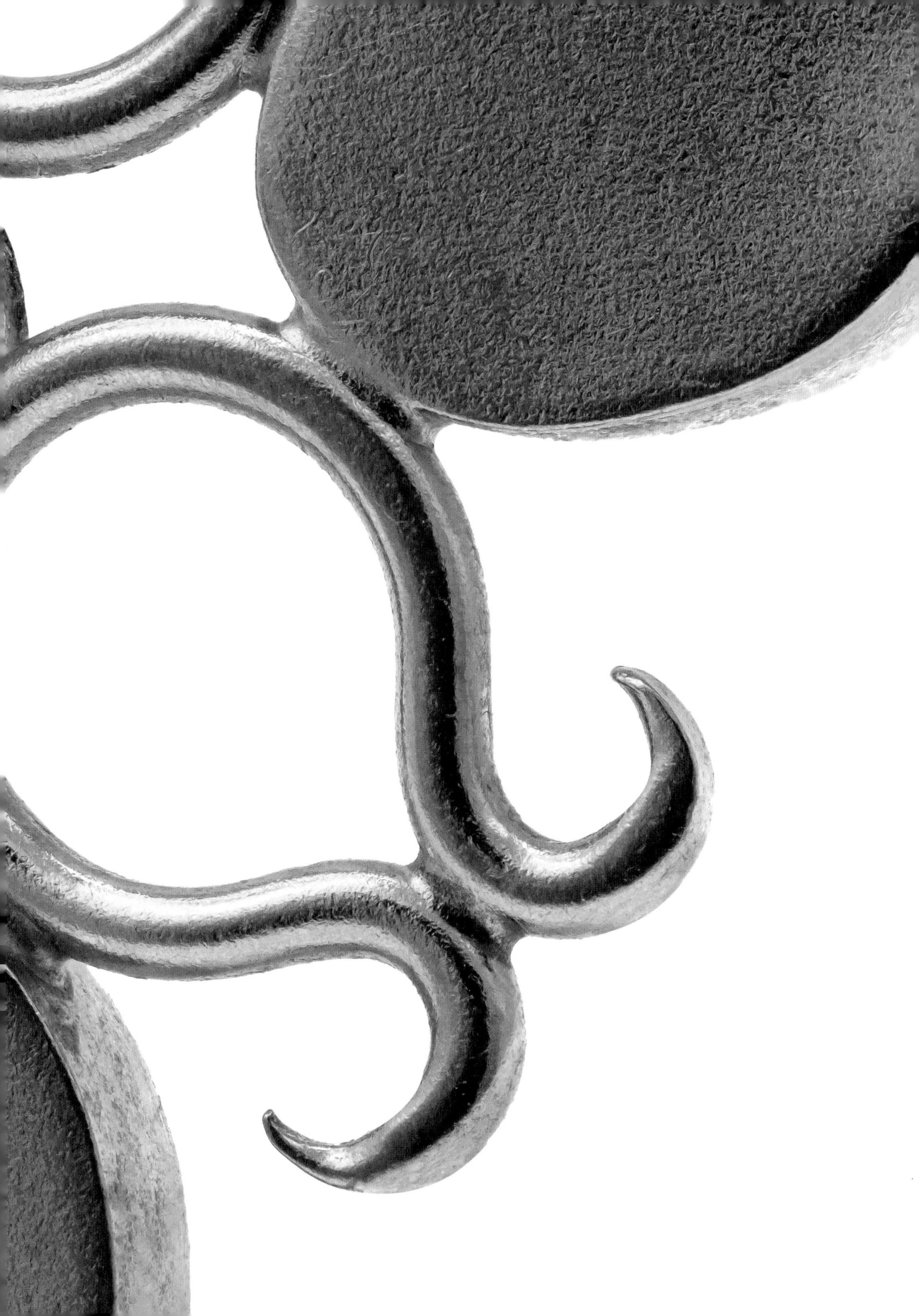

How these techniques come together in this Opal pin:

I soldered my fused bezels to their back sheets up on a tripod using 20k soft solder. Once they were pickled and filed and sanded, I pressed one of the bezels top down into a magnesia block with the gold bar right next to it at the depth I wanted. I used 18k soft solder balls dipped in paste flux and placed them touching both the bezel and the gold bar. I heated both elements equally to melt the solder between them and form an attachment. I repeated this same procedure when I added the other bezel, using the same solder. This piece is a pin, so I used 14k soft solder and the "sandwich" method to attach the pin findings.

It's best to solder a bezel or component to a back sheet from underneath. Dip your solder balls in paste flux and position them around the inner seam. Heat from below with your piece on a tripod & screen to ensures the solder flows only in the seam, not up the side of the bezel.

RIGHT : Heating from below ensures the solder stays in the seam.

WRONG : Heating from above can cause the solder to flow up the bezel.

Vertical seams, such as those on jump rings, bangles, ring shanks and bezel seams, are best soldered by seating them directly on top of a small square of solder on a Solderite board, fluxing them and heating them from above, at 90° to the seam.

RIGHT : Heating from the top will make the solder fill the seam.

WRONG : Heating from the front melts the solder but it likely won't fill the seam.

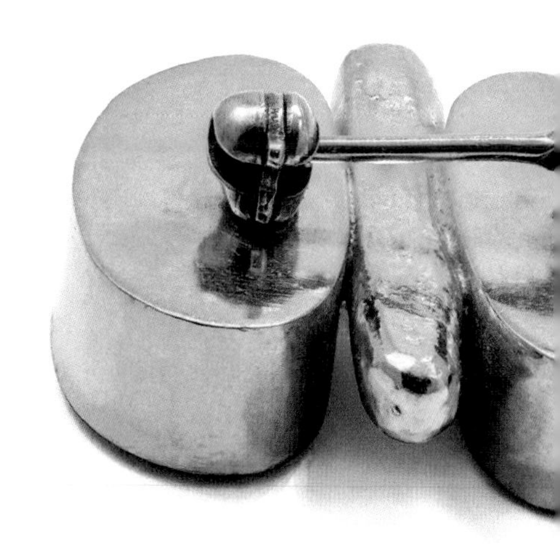

How these techniques come together in this Tourmaline ring:

On the above ring I soldered my fused bezel to the back sheet up on a tripod with 20k soft solder. I soldered my 22k ring shank closed using 20k soft solder using the "vertical seam" method. Once both the shank and the bezel were pickled, filed, and sanded to my satisfaction, I soldered the shank to the bezel using the "wide shank" method. That is, I placed two small balls of 18k soft solder up against the shank on the bezel (see pictures on next page) and heated from across the gap, directly across from the solder. You will use the techniques in this chapter again and again in a thousand variations.

For attaching thick ring shanks, the easiest method is to place solder balls on one side of the seam and heat from the other side, "pulling" the solder through the seam.

RIGHT : Heating both components directly across from the solder will fill the seam.

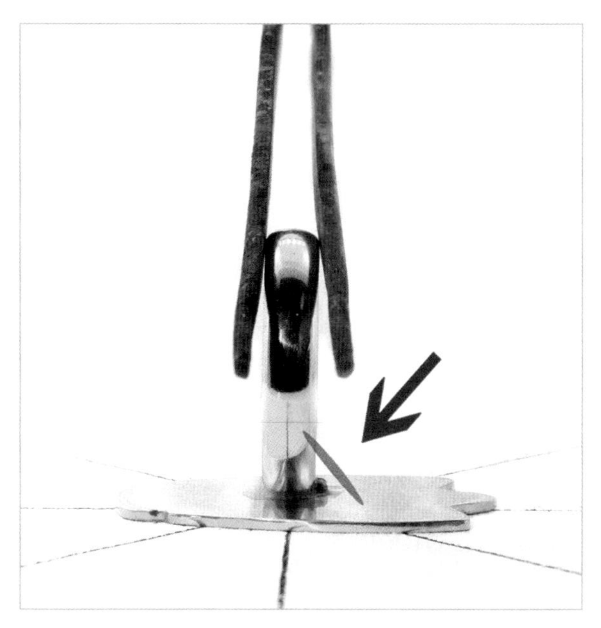

WRONG : Heating the same side as the solder will melt the solder but will not fill the seam.

For soldering a jump ring to a much larger component, you would heat only the larger piece on the side across from the solder to pull the solder through the seam.
(Granulated dome by Savannah Lauren King)

RIGHT : Heating only the larger component directly across from the solder will fill the seam.

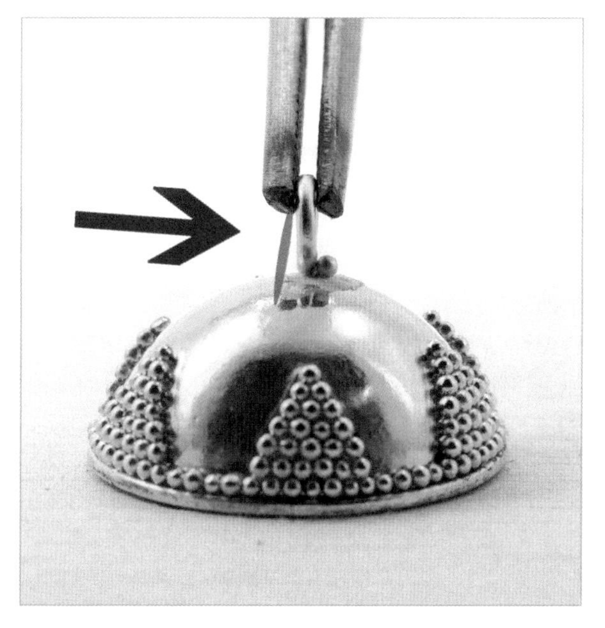

WRONG : Heating the smaller component directly will cause the solder to only attach to the smaller piece.

CHAPTER 6

Use Your Solder Right: More Myths and Realities

SOLDER MYTH #1 – SOLDER WILL NOT FILL GAPS

A seam is a gap. Solder fills seams. Therefore, solder does fill gaps.

It is true, however, that poorly fitted pieces, and big gaps full of solder, make work look sloppy and unprofessional. In addition, while you may eventually be able to plug up a big gap with solder, the larger the gap the harder it is to fill. This is because of the principle of *capillary action*. Capillary action is the ability of a liquid to flow in narrow spaces, often against the flow of gravity. Capillary action is how trees draw water from their roots into their leaves and is also a key factor in how blood moves through our veins.

REALITY CHECK: MAKING CAPILLARY ACTION WORK FOR YOU

In soldering, here's how capillary action works: When solder melts, it becomes a liquid. If your pieces are sanded, filed and fitted together well with as little space as possible, then when you heat your piece, capillary action will pull your liquid solder along your seam and fill it quickly and easily, even if the seam is vertical. The real key is that your solder touches both sides of your seam. If it doesn't, capillary action won't occur. Instead, your solder will only flow on the side of the seam it is touching and make a mess there, without joining the parts. Such messy soldering results in lots of do-overs and extra clean-up, which is tedious and time consuming.

Minimizing gaps is one way to make neat and professional looking pieces that solder well. As you will see in the following diagrams of soldering a bezel to a back sheet, positioning solder correctly, so that it touches both sides of your seam, is another key to making clean, attractive pieces that don't require excessive clean-up. This is the reason solder balls are much more effective than solder squares in many soldering situations. The solder squares tend to shift slightly in the flux and away from contact with both sides. Often, the student does not even notice this has happened. The result is the solder flows but does not flow in the seam where we want it, like this example below ▼. The solder just makes a puddle on whatever surface it is touching. Solder balls tend to "rest" against seams, providing essential contact with both sides of the seam.

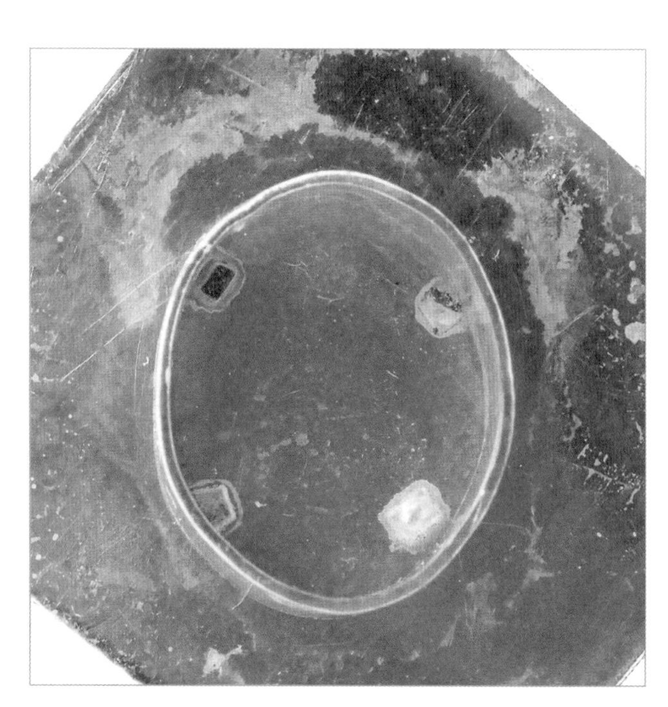

The solder squares have flowed but have not filled the seam.

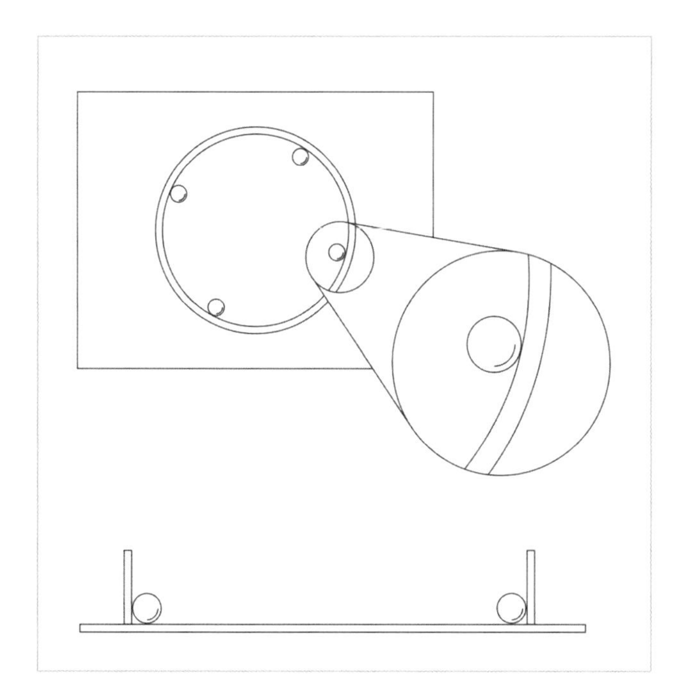

RIGHT : Solder balls "rest" against the seams providing better contact, and the best conditions for capillary action and solder flow.

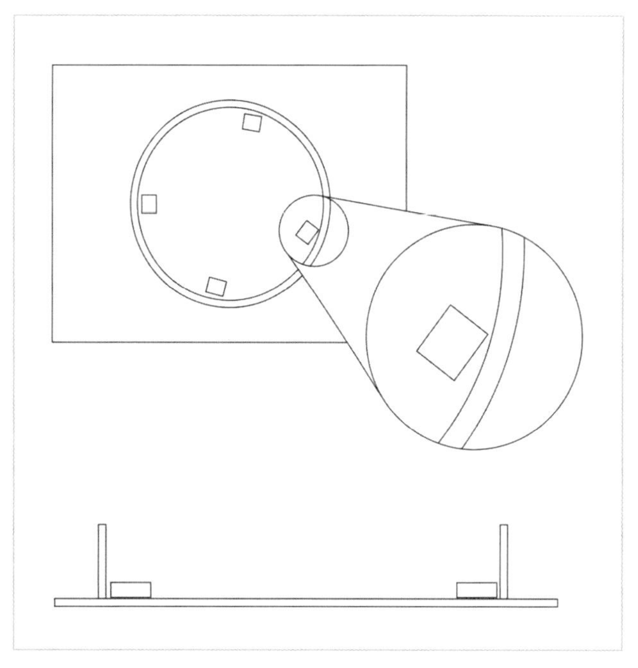

WRONG : Solder squares tend to move out of contact with both sides of the seam, this interferes with capillary action and solder flow.

WHERE TO PUT YOUR SOLDER

In some cases, the easiest way to place your solder to avoid unnecessary clean-up is to make a solder "sandwich," with a chip of solder positioned in the "gap" (i.e., seam) between the two parts you are attaching.

This is my method for putting posts on earrings, and narrow shanks on bezels as well as vertical seams. It's the neatest way to solder these types of jobs because, if you heat the piece correctly, the solder will flow only between the parts being attached, without leaving any scars, bulges or bumps. It does require being certain your parts are in good contact, so I only use it when gravity will help keep everything in contact. I usually rest a pinkie on the third arm when attaching posts and shanks to apply a very small amount of downward pressure. See examples below ▾.

In many cases, however, the solder sandwich method is unstable or impractical. When that is the case, you must place your solder differently, so that it flows across your gap, from one side to the other. In these cases, I use solder balls rather than squares (pallions), which tend to move around more, and leave more of a scar. For example, when I attach an ear wire to an earring or a wide shank to a bezel, I use solder balls. The setup is stable and the clean-up is easy.

To use solder balls, first put the parts in direct contact with each other. Then, add fluxed solder balls on one side of the seam. Finally, heat from the other side of the seam to pull the solder across and fill it up. Remember, the balls must be touching both pieces you are soldering to fill the seam between them. (If not, capillary action won't work and your solder will just make puddles on your piece.) If you use small enough balls that touch both sides of your seam, they will almost disappear when they flow and require little or no clean-up.

Finally, I also consider clean-up when adding more solder to a seam. If I need to reinforce the seam when I solder a wide shank to a bezel, I add more solder balls in the same spot I had previously used, rather than doubling my clean-up work by putting my solder on the opposite side.

HOW MUCH SOLDER TO USE

Using too much solder is another very common problem that also results in messy looking work. Students often use several times as much solder as they need to close a seam. This makes a big, sloppy mess on the piece and, no matter how much time is spent on clean-up, it never looks right. Getting used to manipulating small pieces of solder is essential to making beautiful jewelry. If you have trouble seeing and handling them, there is no shame in using magnifiers or a loupe.

Though solder comes in multiple forms - sheet,

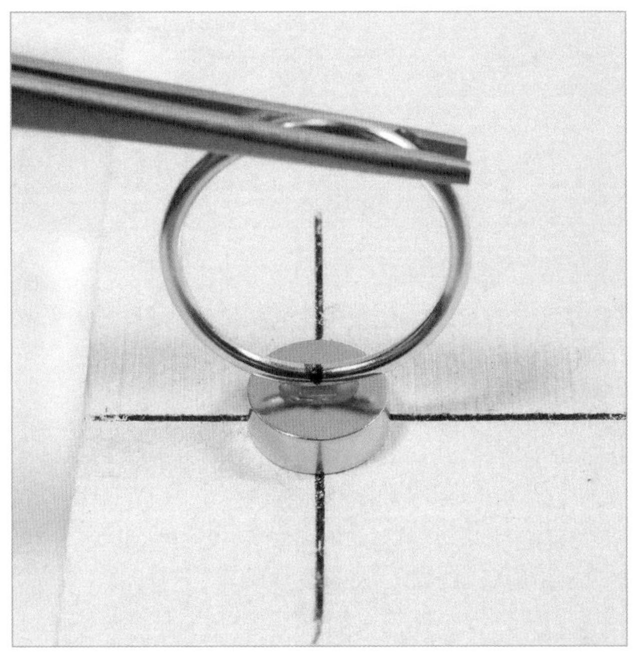

SOLDERING ACROSS A GAP

Make sure the solder balls are touching both the wire and the back sheet.

Notice the tiny solder scars left by this method.

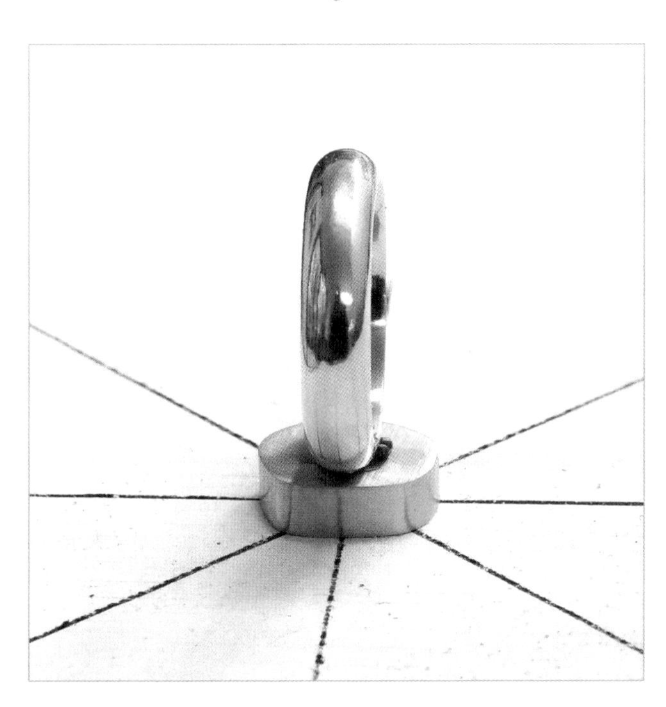

Make sure the solder balls are touching both the shank and bezel.

Minimal solder scarring, little clean-up.

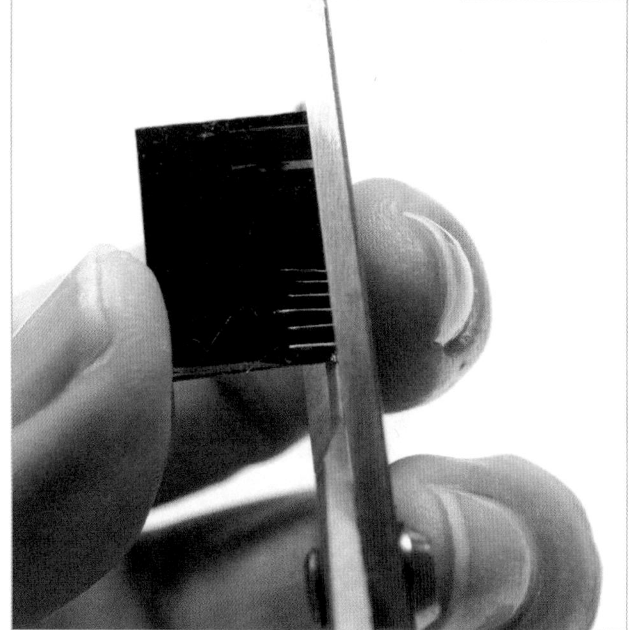

wire, paste, and pre-cut squares - my advice is to buy sheet, mill it as thin as possible, and then cut pieces to the exact size you want. This gives you total control over the amount of solder you use, each time you use it. If you use pre-cut pieces, someone else (who is not working on your piece!) is deciding how much solder you need. There is also a tool that cuts solder into uniform squares, but unless you consistently work on projects that require you to use the exact same size piece of solder every time (and what are the odds of that happening?) what you really get is a bunch of solder squares all cut to the wrong size.

The easiest way to cut your own solder pieces is to cut a fringe first. Then, place the tip of your finger against the outside edge of your fringe (clear of the path of the scissors!) and cut in the opposite direction. If you keep your finger touching the side of the fringe as you cut, your solder will stay put in your work area, rather than flying every which way, see examples above ▲.

Though you won't be getting out your millimeter ruler every time you cut up solder, it is helpful to use a ruler to visualize sizes while you are learning to solder. See example right.

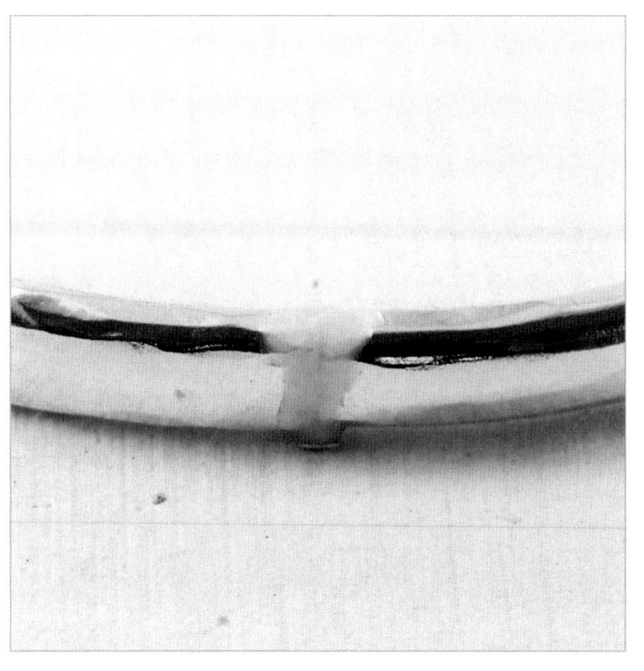

BEFORE SOLDERING
Bangle is 5 mm wide hammered sterling silver wire. Diameter of piece is 70 mm. Hard solder is a 2mm by 3mm rectangle.

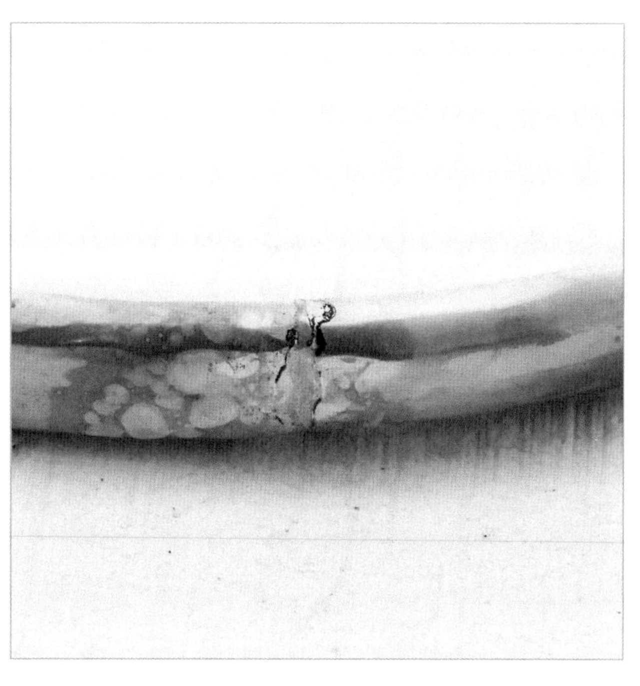

AFTER SOLDERING
Just the right amount to fill the seam with minimal clean-up.

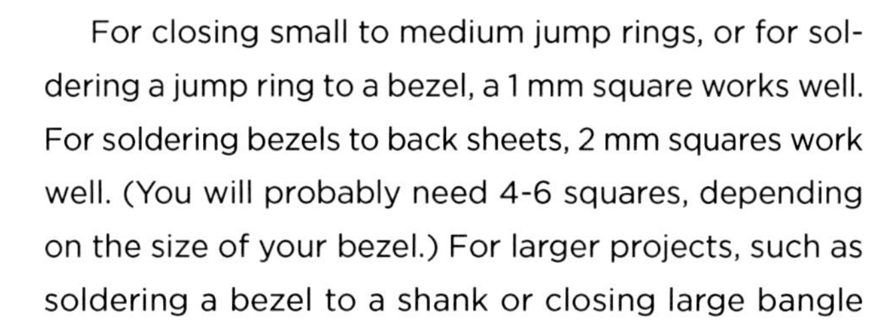

For closing small to medium jump rings, or for soldering a jump ring to a bezel, a 1 mm square works well. For soldering bezels to back sheets, 2 mm squares work well. (You will probably need 4-6 squares, depending on the size of your bezel.) For larger projects, such as soldering a bezel to a shank or closing large bangle bracelet, I would probably use a 2x3 mm rectangle. These are just estimates - each project is different and you will have to be the judge of how much solder to use. Keep in mind that my sizes are based on solder that has been milled as thin as possible. Thicker solder will yield very different results.

USING THE CORRECT AMOUNT OF SOLDER

BEFORE SOLDERING
The jump ring is 18 gauge and 15 mm in diameter. Hard solder square is approximately 1 mm square.

AFTER SOLDERING
Once the solder melts, it is just the right amount to fill the seam so you can sand it without thinning.

BEFORE SOLDERING
The jump ring is 18 gauge and 15 mm in diameter. Hard solder square is approximately 2 mm square.

AFTER SOLDERING
Too much solder! Using this big a piece results in a lump that is time-consuming to clean-up and will never look quite right.

SOLDER MYTH #2 - USE A SOLDER PICK DURING SOLDERING

If I told you the best way to solder is to...

set up your carefully fitted parts in perfect alignment... POKE them with a stick with a GLOB of solder stuck to the point WHILE heating it with a torch AND melt it off the stick exactly into the seam WITHOUT moving any of your parts out of alignment.

What would you say? Probably, "Help!!!" Yet, as far as I'm concerned, this is a fairly accurate description of point soldering. One can probably make almost any technique work with enough practice and patience, but why should you when there are much easier ways?

You may remember from our discussion of tweezers in the Tools section that I recommend keeping a pair of $10-or-less, pointed stone tweezers around for soldering. They are much better than a solder pick for grabbing, placing and moving little bits of solder. Use your tweezers to put your solder where you want it before you turn on your torch, and to gently nudge it back into position if it moves in the flux while heating.

Other books or teachers may have said not to use your tweezers while soldering because the heat will "ruin" them. But I maintain that if you can't solder easily and effectively, having a pristine pair of tweezers in your collection won't do you much good. An occasional "splurge" on a new pair of tweezers is not that expensive when compared with the aggravation and effort it will save you.

Tweezers are great for grabbing and placing solder, and for moving it back into position while heating.

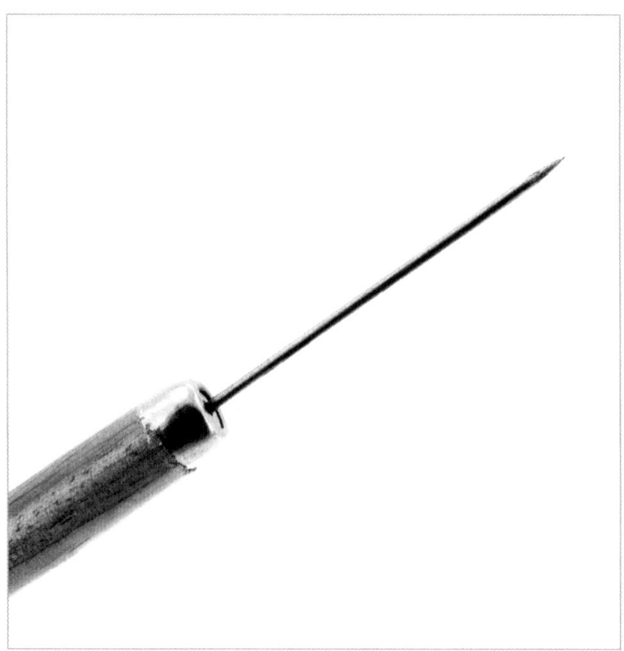

The Point Soldering Tool can't grab or pick up anything, making your job much harder!

CLEAN IT UP RIGHT

If you cleaned your pieces well before soldering, and cut, placed and heated your solder correctly during soldering, you should not have much more to do after soldering than gently sand and polish to restore a shine to your piece. If you do end up with an unsightly bump of solder on your piece (and we all do, sometimes), remember all the tips about finishing from before - namely:

1

File your solder bump carefully and evenly with a fine (#2 cut) file and blend the filed area in with the rest of the piece. Pay close attention so you don't dig a trench into your piece or make deep scratches with the file.

2

Sand out your file marks. Don't change to finer sandpaper until you have taken out every possible scratch you can with coarser sandpaper.

3

Remember that filing, sanding and polishing are all just progressive steps in the process of removing larger visible scratches, and replacing them with a surface of smaller scratches until they are invisible to the naked eye. If you don't like a high shine on your pieces, that's fine, but it's no excuse for sloppiness - you cannot leave random bumps and scratches on your piece if you aspire to making fine jewelry.

If you pay close attention to these tips, and to the other techniques in this book, I promise you can make beautiful jewelry quicker, easier and better than before. The tutorials that follow will give you more detail about specific and common scenarios you may encounter during your jewelry making.

TUTORIAL 1

Soldering A Vertical Seam

Vertical seams are extremely common in jewelry making. You will encounter them when closing bezels, ring shanks, jump rings and bangle bracelets, to name a just a few examples. You can use the procedure below to solder any type of vertical seam. All that will vary is the size of the torch tip and the amount of solder you use.

STEP 1

Shut your seam tightly. Remember, capillary action will draw your liquid solder up a tightly butted seam effortlessly, but will not work if you have a significant gap. Hold your seam up to a light source and check it. If you see much light shining through, re-butt the seam until the gap is completely closed.

STEP 2

Cut a small square of solder, dip it in paste flux and place your seam over it (this is one of the few times a solder square works better than a ball). Make sure the solder square is touching both sides of your seam. This is very important. If the solder is only touching one side, it will make a messy puddle there, rather than flowing into the seam.

STEP 3

Use your tweezers to add a small amount of paste flux to the seam.

STEP 4

Heat from above, holding flame directly over the seam at 90° (see photos). Do not heat the whole piece. Use the end of the flame to solder, rather than the blue cone.

STEP 5

Pull away as soon as the solder flows up to the top the seam. If your seam is tightly butted, this happens almost instantly once your solder flows. You will want to watch the solder carefully and pull away as soon as it flows to avoid melting your piece or overheating the solder so much it leaves pits in your metal.

The most common mistake students make when soldering vertical seams...

is not checking carefully enough that both sides of the seam are actually touching the solder. This requires getting down at eye level with your solder. The situation may look very different from this perspective as opposed to when viewed from above.

WARNING

Do not position the cone of the flame close to your seam. Since you have the Solderite board bouncing the flame's heat back onto your piece, you needn't worry about your heat dissipating (as you do when you use the tripod and screen). The tricky part here is your reaction time. Although you can certainly get the solder to flow with this setup, the problem often comes once the solder has flowed. The natural instinct is to pull the flame back up, not off to the side, adding a few seconds of reaction time - a lot of time when soldering! If you do not cease heating as soon as the solder has flowed where you want it, it will continue to flow, possibly to where you do not want it. Practice pulling your flame off to the side to get the heat off your piece right away, rather than pulling it upwards and use the tip, not the cone of the flame.

RIGHT
Hold end of flame at 90° to the seam.

WRONG
The blue cone is too close to the seam to solder safely.

SOLDERING VERTICAL SEAMS

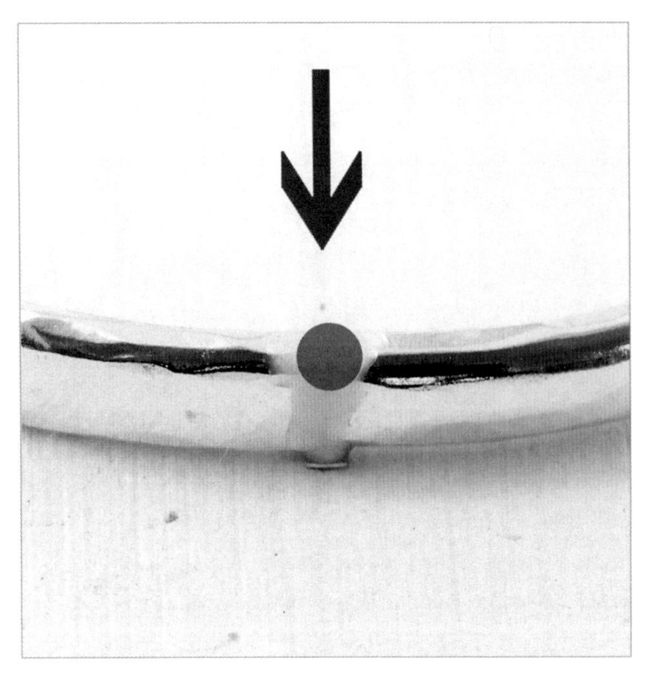

BEFORE SOLDERING

Bangle is 5 mm wide hammered sterling silver wire. Diameter is 70 mm. Use a 1 tip and hard silver solder.

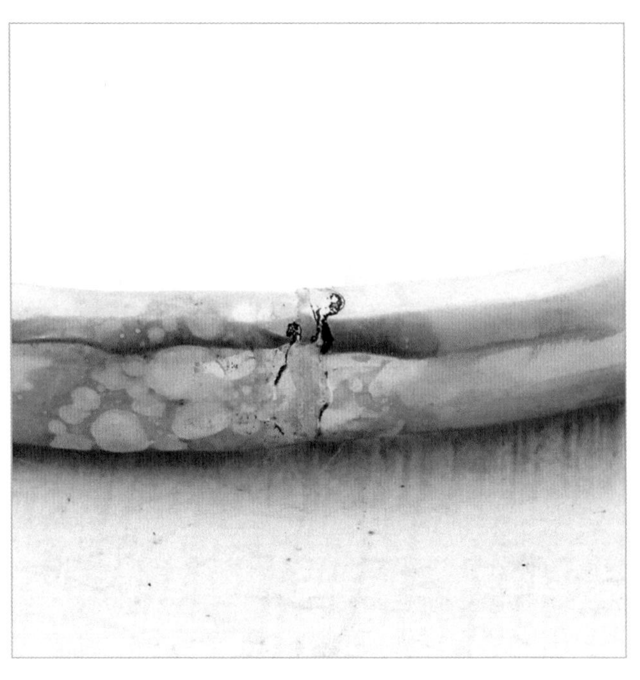

AFTER SOLDERING

Bangle seam after soldering.

BEFORE SOLDERING

Jump ring is 20 gauge round wire, 20 karat gold. Diameter is 3 mm. Use a 00 tip and 20k soft gold solder. For silver, use hard solder.

AFTER SOLDERING

Jump ring after soldering.

BEFORE SOLDERING

Ring shank is 4.5 mm wide half round wire, 22 karat gold. Size 6. Use a 0 tip and 20k soft gold solder. For silver, use hard solder.

AFTER SOLDERING

Ring shank after soldering and pickling. Only a small amount of clean-up will be needed.

TUTORIAL 2

Soldering a Bezel to a Back Sheet

STEP 1

Flatten your back sheet. The easiest way is to anneal it, let it air cool (quenching it causes it to warp and become harder to flatten), and then press it between two clean steel blocks. Do not twist or corkscrew the blocks together or you will grind any dirt or dust present on your block into your piece. As an alternative method, you can use a rawhide mallet to hammer in small counterclockwise circles as you go around the piece, also in a counterclockwise direction, see diagram of this hammering method to the right ›. One of my instructors showed me this technique years ago and it's quite miraculous. I'm sure it has something to do with how the molecules spread outward but the important thing is that it always works.

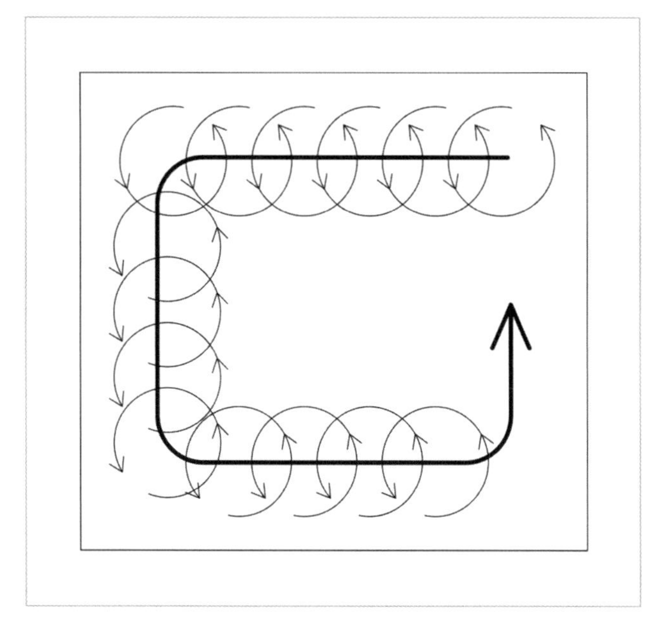

STEP 2

Sand your bezel. First, sand out any visible seam where you soldered or fused your bezel shut. Then sand the bottom of the bezel completely flat on a piece of sandpaper you have laid on level, clean work surface. You can also sand the top of your bezel if it is a regular shape (round, square, oval, etc.), but if it is an irregular shape it is best to just sand the bottom. The unsanded top will let you know which side is up so you don't accidentally solder the wrong side down.

STEP 3

Place the bezel on top of the back sheet and double check that you have a nice fit with no significant gaps. Make sure you have considered any decorative elements you may want to add onto the back sheet around the bezel to ensure you have enough room for them.

STEP 4

Make several small solder balls and use your stone tweezers to dip them in paste flux and place them inside the bezel. The balls must make contact with both the bezel and the back sheet if they are to flow properly and fill the seam. My bezels are fused 22k gold and my back sheets are 20k gold so I will use 20k soft solder. If you were working in sterling silver, brass, or copper you would solder your bezel closed with hard (using the vertical seam method) and then use medium to solder the bezel to the back sheet.

STEP 5

Place your bezel and back sheet on top of the screen on a tripod.

STEP 6

Select an appropriate size tip. For most bezels and back sheets, a 0 or 1 tip will suffice. A 0 tip is better for small jobs on silver pieces, while a 1 tip is better for larger jobs on high-karat gold, which require more heat. If it's a toss-up, it's generally better to use the larger tip so you can solder hot and fast. You just need to make

RIGHT : This torch position will help the solder flow quickly.

WRONG : This torch position is letting a lot of torch heat escape beyond the piece. This can cause solder to oxidize and fail to flow.

sure you are paying close attention so when the solder flows you pull away immediately.

STEP 7

Position your flame's tip directly on your back sheet as you heat from beneath. Keep the flame steady – if you circle or bob and weave, your heat will dissipate and the solder may not flow. Pull away as soon as you see the solder travel all the way around the bezel.

STEP 8

Cool and pickle; then check for gaps. If you see any, add more solder balls with paste flux and heat again until seam is completely full.

THE BEST WAY TO SOLDER A BEZEL TO A BACK SHEET

Place the cleaned bezel on the back sheet, distribute small balls of solder dipped in paste flux so they touch both the bezel and back sheet.

Place piece on top of tripod screen and heat from below until you see the solder flow, then pull away the flame.

The bezel and back sheet after soldering.

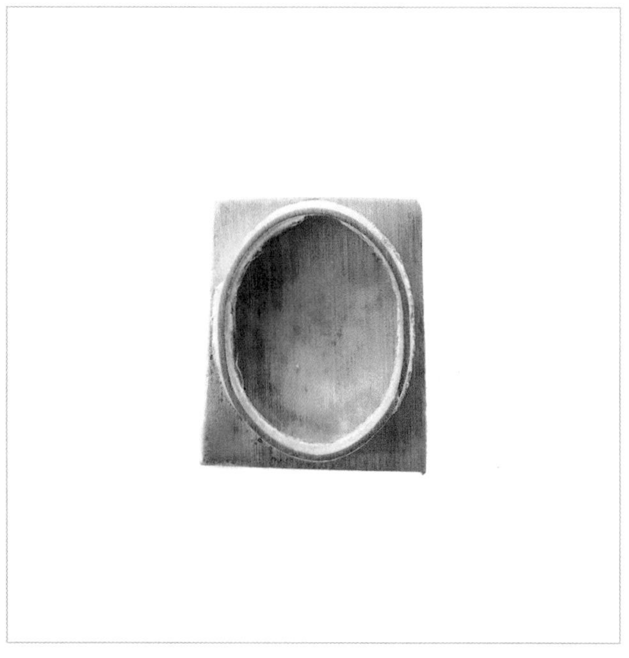

The bezel and back sheet after pickling.

TUTORIAL 3

Soldering a Wide Shank to a Bezel

STEP 1

Clean-up and pre-polish both your bezel and shank.

STEP 2

File a flat onto the shank where you will join it to the bezel. Check to see whether you can sit the shank on the back of the bezel without using the third arm to hold it. If you can do this, you know you have filed flat and will have good contact and a sturdy seam. If you cannot, you must keep filing until the shank can stand up on its own. This way you assure yourself your shank is filed straight and possibly avoid using the third arm when you solder, which makes the job a lot easier.

STEP 3

Using a Solderite board with X and Y-axes drawn onto it (see Get in Line! The Best Soldering Tip Ever for more on this). Center the bezel on the axes and then center the shank on the bezel.

STEP 4

Dip one or two small balls of solder in paste flux and place them against the shank on the back of the bezel, on the side farthest away from you. I have used only 20k soft gold solder so far, so I will use 18k soft gold solder. For silver, use medium or easy solder.

STEP 5

Heat from the opposite side from the solder using a 0 tip. Angle your flame so it hits both the bezel and the shank. Hold the flame steady until you see the solder flow and fill the seam.

STEP 6

Cool and pickle; then check to make sure the seam is completely filled. If you see gaps, add more solder to the same spot as before to minimize your clean-up.

THE BEST WAY TO SOLDER A WIDE SHANK TO A BEZEL

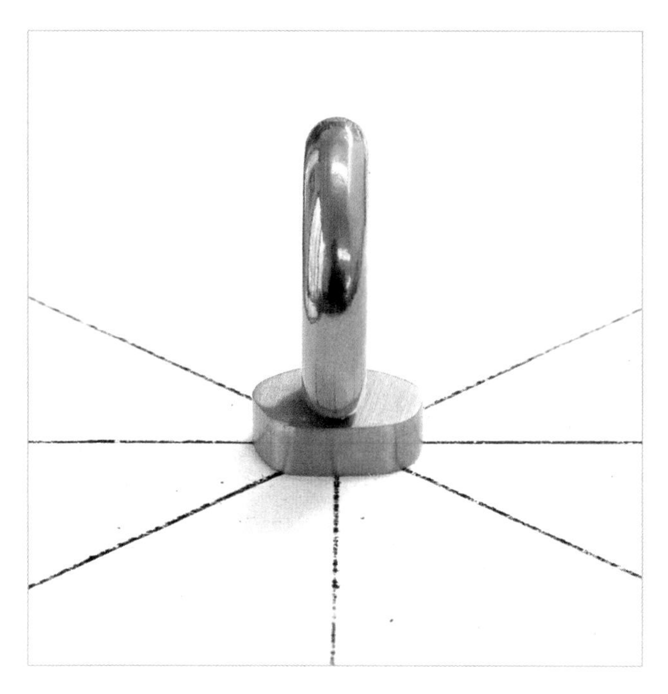

Use the axis on the Solderite board to center the shank on the bezel.

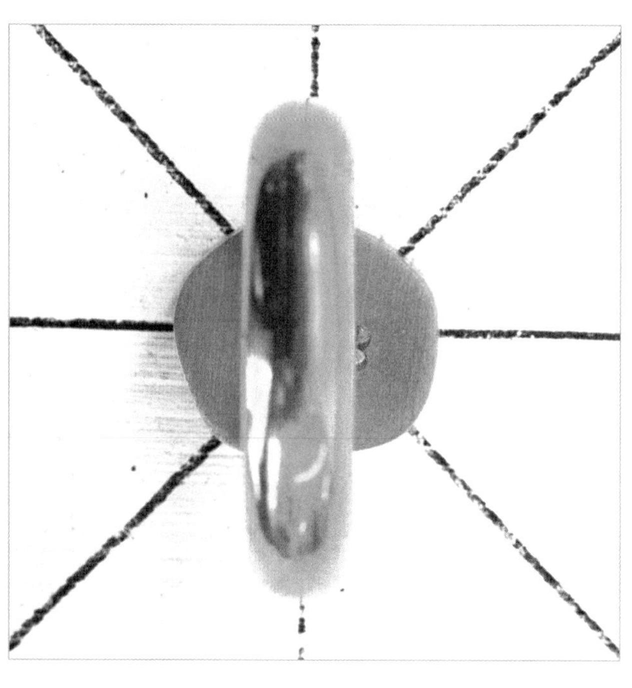

Dip and place your solder balls on the side farthest from you.

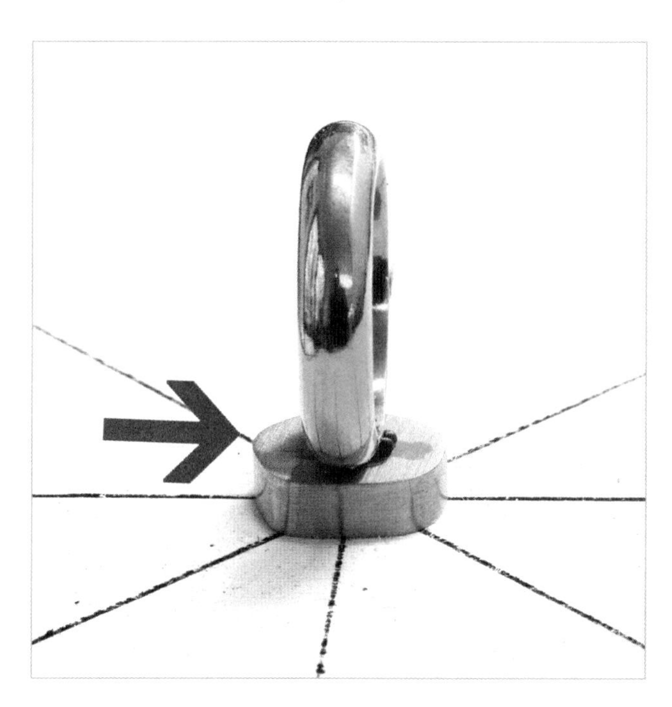

Heat from the opposite side, positioning the flame so it hits both the bezel and the bottom of the shank.

Note the minimal solder scar and easy clean-up left by this method.

TUTORIAL 4

Soldering a Narrow Shank to a Bezel

STEP 1

Make sure your bezel and shank are completely clean and scratch free.

STEP 2

Draw X and Y-axes on your Solderite board to help you line up your piece (see Get in Line! The Best Soldering Tip Ever for more on how to do this).

STEP 3

Using your pre-drawn axis, center your bezel. Dip a rectangular piece of solder (this is a situation that calls for a somewhat larger piece of solder than usual since you are just using one) into paste flux and center it on the back of the bezel. I have used 20k soft on the shank and to solder the bezel to the back sheet so we will step down to 18k soft gold solder. For silver, use medium or easy solder. If you are making a stacking ring, rather than a stand-alone ring, place your shank 1/3 up or down on the Y-Axis, as rings with the shank soldered dead center do not stack as well.

STEP 4

Mark the shank's original seam using a Sharpie® marker so that it is easy for you to see. Use a third arm to grasp the shank at the top edge and align the seam of the shank exactly over the solder chip. Lower the shank until you feel it is firmly positioned atop the solder square (see Put Your Solder in the Right Place for more on this "sandwich" method of soldering). Do not file a flat on the shank if you are making a stack ring as this will make the rings stack less attractively.

STEP 5

Get up and walk around the piece to check the shank from all angles. You may think it's perpendicular and appropriately positioned from the front, but it may look very different when viewed from the side.

STEP 6

Using a 0 tip, heat while angling the flame at both the bezel and the base of the shank. Hold the flame steady until you see the solder flow and fill the seam. Try to use your non-dominant hand to hold the torch, and rest your pinky on top of the tweezers in the third arm. That way, you can feel the contact between the bezel and the shank.

STEP 7

Cool and pickle; then check your connection. If necessary, use a small ball of solder to augment your seam while holding the shank in position with the third arm.

THE BEST WAY TO SOLDER A NARROW SHANK TO A BEZEL

Use the axes on the Solderite board to line up your solder chip and bezel.

Position the shank's original seam directly over the solder.

Heat from the front, positioning flame on both shank and bezel.

The pickled ring needs no clean-up and is ready for stone setting.

TUTORIAL 5

Soldering Links in a Chain

STEP 1

Make links of the desired size by coiling wire tightly around a dowel or rod. Saw carefully through coil to create flush joints.

STEP 2

Divide your links into two equal groups. Butt one group closed and solder shut using the vertical seam technique in Tutorial 1. My links are 20k gold so I will use 20k soft gold solder. Students working in sterling silver, brass or copper should use hard silver solder. Hard or medium silver solder works better on brass and copper than any other solder I have seen. Having the chain plated at the end of the project in the respective metal will hide the color differences beautifully. Pickle and re-round soldered links. Sand any excess solder from joints.

STEP 3

Use your pliers to twist open the other half of your links. If you twist to open them, rather than pulling them apart into oval shapes, you will distort them less and have a much easier time butting them back together later. Anneal and pickle the open links.

STEP 4

Thread an open link through two of your soldered ones. Carefully close the open ring and butt together the seam with your chain nose pliers.

STEP 5

Set your links up on a Solderite board, positioning the seam of the open link far away as possible from contact with your other links. If you need more tension to keep your links apart, press a straight pin or binding wire through the closed links into the soldering board. Using this method means it is safe to use the same solder again to close the rest of the links.

STEP 6

Dip a small (1mm or smaller) square of solder into paste flux and place on top of the seam of the open link. Check very carefully that the solder is touching both sides of the seam. If it is not, it will melt and make a mess on one side of your link, rather than filling in the seam.

STEP 7

Using a 00 tip, position your flame at 90° to the soldering board, just a tiny bit in front of the seam. When the solder flows, it will be drawn into the seam.

STEP 8

Repeat all the way down the chain, threading an open link through the closed link at the end of the chain, and then through another closed link. If you want to solder the chain in the most efficient way, interweave all the open and closed links first and then solder all the open links shut. When all the links are soldered, pickle and sand off any excess solder. Tumbling the chain will harden it and give it a bright, shiny finish.

IF YOUR LINKS ARE:

22k Gold use 20k Soft Gold Solder

20k Gold use 20k Soft Gold Solder

18k Gold use 18k Soft Gold Solder

14k Gold use 14k Soft Gold Solder

10k Gold use 10k Soft Gold Solder

Sterling Silver use Hard Silver Solder

Brass use Hard Silver Solder

Copper use Hard Silver Solder

TIP : If you twist your links to open them, they will be much easier to butt closed.

Close and solder half your links with small pieces of 20k soft gold solder.

SOLDERING LINKS TOGETHER

Set up your links on the Solderite board. Place a small (1 mm or less) solder chip over the seam so it touches both sides of the link.

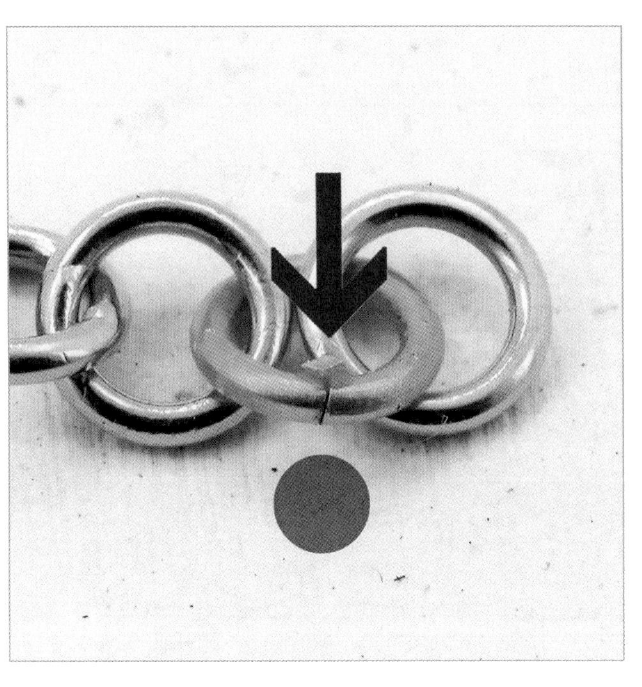

Heat at 90° to the seam, positioning the flame over and a little bit in front of it, until the solder flows.

This is what the seam looks like once the solder has flowed.

A few swipes with fine sandpaper is all the seam needs to be finished.

TUTORIAL 6

Soldering on an Ear Wire

STEP 1

Roll your ear wire gently between two clean steel blocks to straighten. Don't press too hard or slam the blocks together or you can create flat spots on the wire.

STEP 2

Use the lines on your Solderite board to set the wire straight on your piece. Avoid using the third arm, as it is usually more trouble than it's worth for this kind of soldering.

STEP 3

Make sure the wire is making good contact everywhere along the piece. If it's not, you may need to straighten your wire or adjust the height of your piece before you proceed.

STEP 4

Dip small solder balls (which leave less of a scar than squares) in paste flux and place against the wire on the side farthest away from you. It is preferable to use a very small amount of solder and add a little more later than to use too much and have to clean it up. The more you solder, the better you will get at accurately estimating how much to use. Since my leaf is 22k gold and my ear wires are 20k gold, I could use 20k soft solder. However, I have found when attaching a finding to a piece it is often safer to step down the solder a bit. I will use 18k soft gold solder. For silver, use medium or easy solder.

STEP 5

Use a 00 tip to heat the piece (NOT the ear wire) from above at a 90° angle. The solder will flow towards the heat and under the ear wire. As soon as you see the solder flow along the length of the wire, pull the flame away.

STEP 6

Cool and pickle the piece. Double check that the solder has flowed completely along the length of the ear wire, with no gaps or opening. If you need to fill an opening, add more solder using the method above. Add the solder from the same side as before to minimize clean-up later.

SOLDERING DOWN THE EAR WIRE

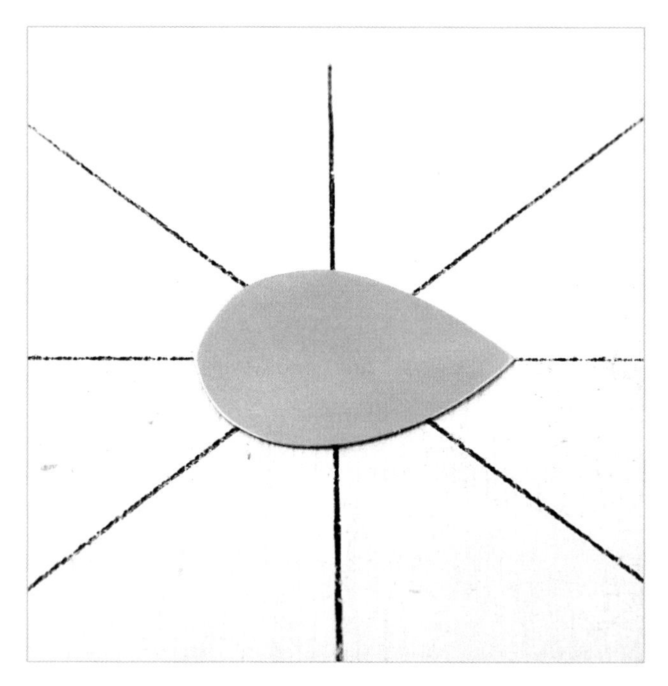

Use the axes on the Solderite board to line up the ear wire.

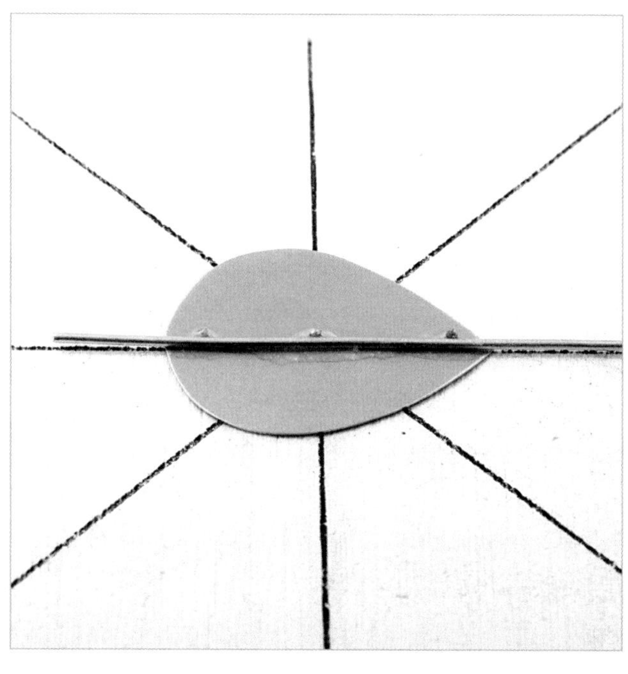

Dip very small balls of solder (1 mm) in paste flux and position against the wire. Make sure the balls touch both the wire and the piece during soldering.

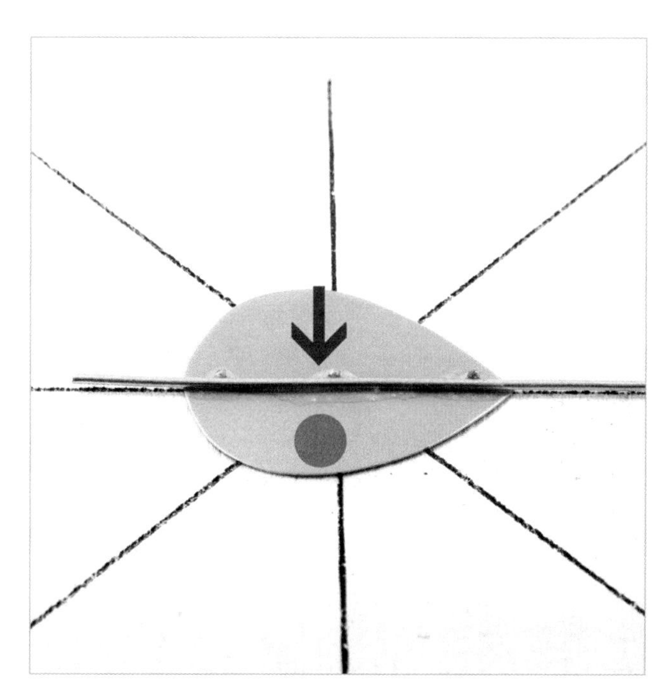

Heat from above, keeping the flame at 90° to the piece. Keep the flame positioned on the piece, not the ear wire.

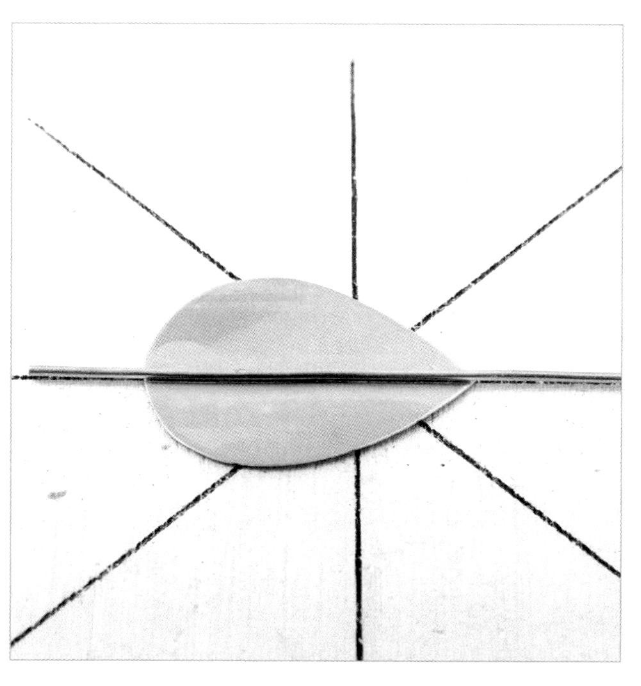

This method results in very tiny solder scars that can be quickly cleaned up.

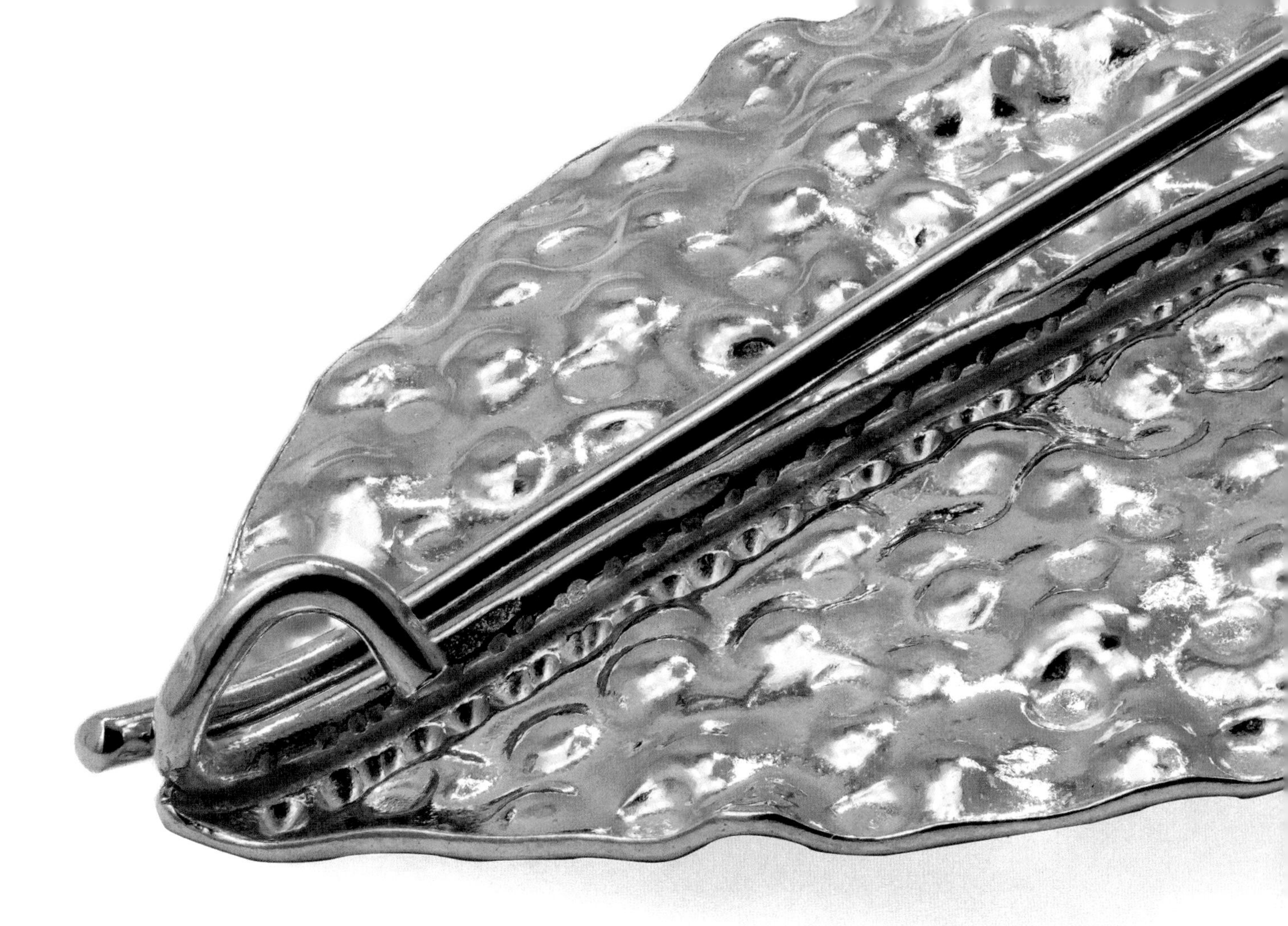

TUTORIAL 7

Soldering a Post to a Bezel

STEP 1

Sand and polish all components before soldering.

STEP 2

Double check that your bezel is level. If not, now is the time to fix it.

STEP 3

Cut a small square of solder, only slightly larger than the area of the bottom of the post. This is one of the times you want a square, not a solder ball.

STEP 4

Use your tweezers to dip your solder square in paste flux and place it exactly where you want to solder your post. I use 14k soft gold solder whether my posts are 14k or 18k gold. For silver, use easy solder. For earrings up to 5 or 6 mm long you can place your post dead center. For larger earrings you will want to place your post a little above the center, otherwise they won't hang correctly on the ear.

STEP 5

Use your third arm to grasp the post at the very top, as far away from where you will be soldering as possible. If you have trouble grasping the post, file a little groove into your cross locking tweezers to hold it straight.

STEP 6

Center your post directly over your solder with good contact between them. Many jewelers who use thicker and/or harder metals than I do will drill a small hole, half melt a tiny bit of solder in the hole and then set up the post and reflow. Whether you are drilling a hole or soldering directly to the back sheet as I do, the following steps will insure soldering success.

STEP 7

Get up and walk around the piece to check the post from all angles. You may think it's perpendicular and appropriately positioned from the front, but it may look very different when viewed from the side.

STEP 8

Heat while aiming the flame at the bezel, NOT the post. Because it is small, the post can overheat and melt very quickly. Remember that, when heating objects of very different sizes, you must concentrate your heat on the larger object to avoid melting the smaller one.

STEP 9

Use your non-dominant hand to hold the torch, and rest the pinkie of your dominant hand on top of the tweezers in the third arm. That way, you can press down ever so slightly when the solder becomes liquid, ensuring good contact between the bezel and the post. Watch the solder closely and pull the flame upward for one little flick when it flows to ensure a nice collar of solder around the base of the post. The proper technical name for this is the meniscus, see picture below ▼.

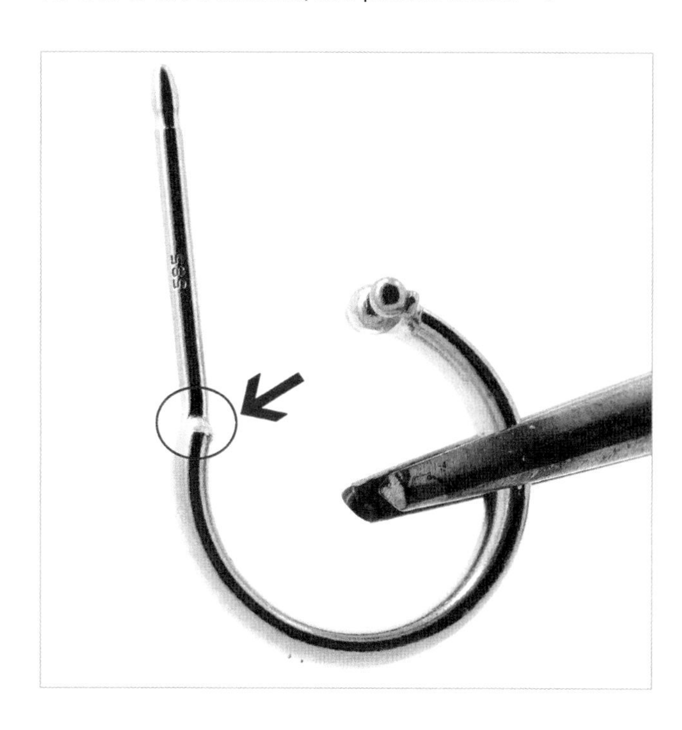

The Meniscus

THE BEST WAY TO SOLDER ON A POST

Dip a solder square into paste flux and place it where you want the post to go.

Use a third arm to position the post in the center of the solder square. Keep the flame pointed at the bezel while heating.

The solder joint after soldering.

The solder joint after pickling. This kind of seam requires no clean-up.

TUTORIAL 8

Soldering a Jump Ring to a Bezel

STEP 1

Sand and polish all components before soldering.

STEP 2

Decide where you want the jump ring to be positioned on the bezel. You may want it aligned with the back edge of the bezel, or you may want it positioned closer to the middle of the bezel (this is usually done when the bezel is high and dangling elements won't hang correctly if you position the jump ring at the back edge of the bezel).

STEP 3

OPTION A

If you want your jump ring positioned at the back edge of the bezel, use your Solderite board. Place your bezel facing up and center it using the axes on your board. Then proceed to STEP 4.

OPTION B

If you want the jump ring positioned toward the middle of the bezel, use a Magnesia block instead of a Solderite board. Since you can't draw as well on the Magnesia block, use a scribe to mark X and Y-axes on your block so you can center your bezel and your jump ring. Then mark a line on your bezel where you want your jump ring and press the bezel top down into the block up to this line. Line up your jump ring with the bezel and proceed to STEP 4.

STEP 4

Dip a small (about 1mm) solder ball in paste flux and place on top of the jump ring, resting against the bezel. Since I have used 20k soft solder to close my jump ring and solder my bezel to the back sheet, I will step down to 18k soft gold solder. In silver, use medium solder. Make sure there is no space between the jump ring and bezel. If the bezel keeps moving away from you as you are positioning the jump ring, you can press a binding wire pin or straight pin into the block above the bezel to secure it.

STEP 5

Position the 00 tip parallel to the block. Aim it at the bezel, right next to the jump ring.

STEP 6

Pull the flame away immediately when the solder flows between the two.

STEP 7

Cool and pickle the piece. Before declaring the task complete, double check that there is a sturdy connection between the bezel and the jump ring.

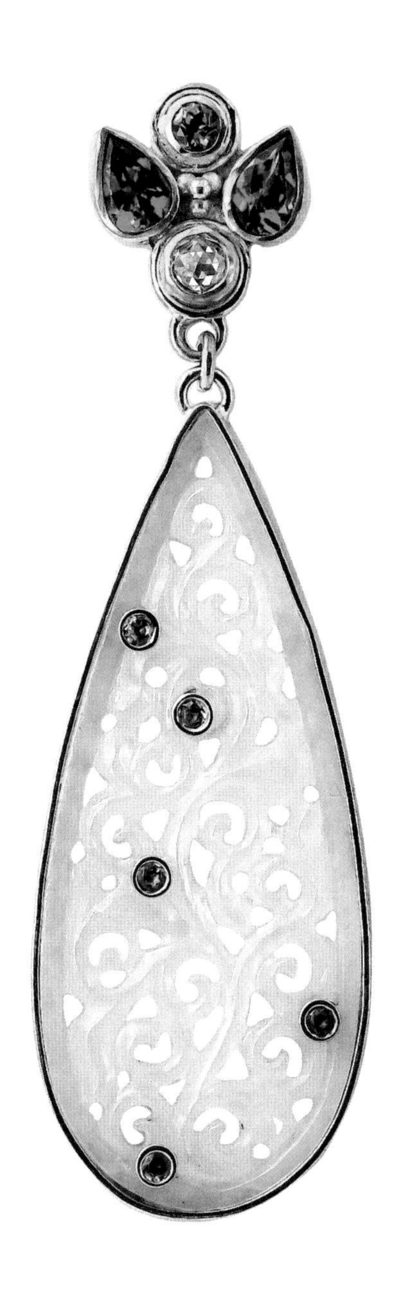
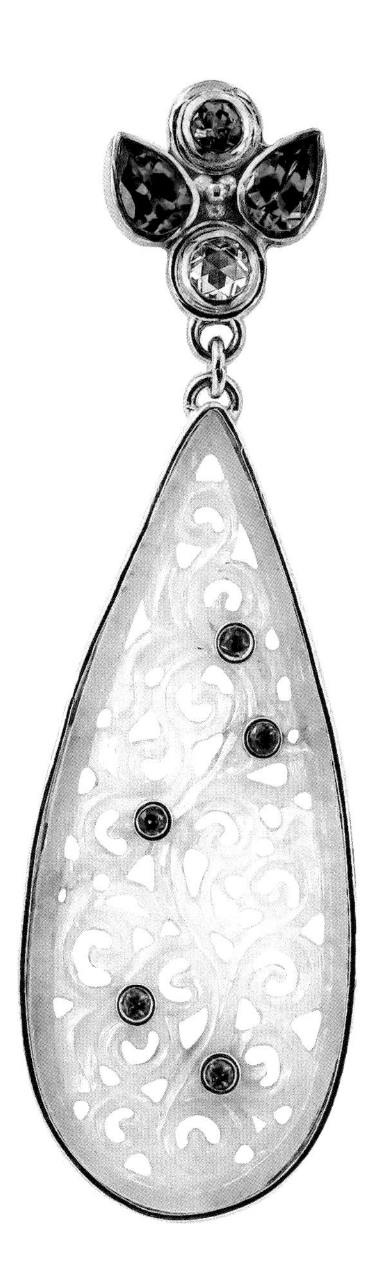

SOLDERING A JUMP RING TO A LOW BEZEL

Once the bezel and jump ring are sanded and cleaned, align them using the axes on the block.

Dip a small ball of solder in paste flux and place on top of the jump ring, resting against the bezel.

Position the flame parallel to the soldering board, hitting the bezel right next to, but not on, the jump ring.

This kind of seam requires little to no clean-up.

SOLDERING A JUMP RING TO A TALL BEZEL

Make a mark at the height you want your jump ring.

Press your bezel into the Magnesia block to the appropriate depth and line it up using the axes scribed on your block.

Dip the solder ball in paste flux and place it on top of the jump ring, resting against the bezel.

Heat the area right next to the jump ring so the solder will be drawn into the seam.

In Conclusion

Jewelry Arts Institute is an amazing laboratory for me. Here, I have learned from teaching metalsmithing for the past two decades that there are many different ways to apply a technique. Soldering is the most important and least understood technique. I wrote this book to show not only the concepts of soldering but to teach the easiest, fastest, and most reliable methods for achieving the best results no matter the design of the piece or the metals used to create it. I now challenge you to take these insights and use them as a means to discover your best and most creative work. Happy Soldering!

Glossary

ACETYLENE
The hottest-burning common fuel gas.

ANNEAL
To heat metal to make it more malleable.

BACK SHEET
Any piece of flat sheet onto which components are soldered.

BEZEL
A strip of metal used for setting stones and enamels.

BRASS
A metal alloy made of copper and zinc.

BRAZING
The correct but mostly unused term for how jewelers solder.

CAPILLARY ACTION
The movement of a liquid along narrow spaces caused by the attraction of molecules. This scientific principle explains how water is drawn up from the ground into tree trunks, blood moves in our veins, and solder easily flows against gravity to fill small gaps.

FERROUS METAL
Metal containing iron, e.g., steel.

FINDING
Term used for posts, ear wires, clasps or anything you attach to jewelry so it can be worn.

FIRE SCALE
Cuprous oxide or a reddish purple "stain" that forms beneath the surface of silver. Caused by the combination of copper and oxygen.

GRIT BOWL
Metal dish filled with some form of carborundum grit, meant to be used for soldering (which I do not recommend except in rare cases).

HEAT SINK
Any object, usually made of steel, that is used to draw heat away from components or previously flowed solder seams that need protection from heat.

JUMP RING
Common term for a circle of wire used to make chain or form attachments.

OCHRE
A clay-based soil used to deliberately make solder seams dirty and prevent solder from flowing or re-flowing.

OXIDATION
Cupric oxide or the black surface that develops on copper-containing alloys (such as gold alloys, sterling silver, brass and copper) when they are heated. Removed by pickling.

PALLIONS or SOLDER PALLIONS
Solder squares. I use the term squares rather than pallions.

PASTE FLUX
A fluoride/borate type flux. More concentrated than liquid flux. Fluorides in large doses can be toxic, so don't eat it or inhale deeply while heating it.

PASTE SOLDER
A combination of paste flux and solder filings.

PICKLE
An acid bath used to remove oxides and spent flux from a piece once it has been soldered. We at JAI use sodium bisulfate (PH minus) but other studios use citric acid or commercially prepared pickles. The common name "pickle" has been retained from olden days, when jewelers often used salt and one of the more easily obtainable forms of acid, vinegar, to clean their jewelry after soldering.

SHANK
Ring band or the part of the ring that circles the finger.

SODIUM BISULFATE
An acid salt used in solution to clean metal after soldering.

SOLDER
A metal that melts at a lower temperature to attach metals with a higher melting point.

SOLDERING
The act of heating a metal with a lower melting point to join metals with a higher melting point.

SOLDERING PICK or POINT SOLDERING TOOL
A pointed tool, possibly invented by the Devil, intended to place solder while heating. I recommend tweezers instead of a soldering pick.

STRIKER
Metal tool with a flint, used to create sparks for lighting the torch.

THIRD ARM
A movable stand with a cross-locking tweezers attached to it.

TRIPOD
A three legged soldering stand used with a screen.

[1] Since the Sharpie® marker people have not tested their products at the temperature range I suggest they requested I publish this disclaimer: Sanford, L.P., the registered owner of the Sharpie trademark, has not independently verified the accuracy of this statement.

About the Author

Jeanette K Caines has been making jewelry for over twenty years or since the jewelry gods told her she should lead the charge in not only making, but teaching others how to make pieces that are beautiful and inspiring. She is the director of Jewelry Arts Institute, the leading jewelry school in New York City and her pieces can be found in private collections everywhere.

Made in the USA
San Bernardino, CA
16 March 2020

65797272R00069